Practical Management and Leadership for Doctors

Practical Management and Leadership for Doctors

Second Edition

John Wattis
School of Human and Health Science
University of Huddersfield
Huddersfield, England

Stephen Curran
School of Human and Health Sciences
University of Huddersfield
Huddersfield, England
and
Consultant in Old Age Psychiatry
South West Yorkshire Partnership NHS Foundation Trust
Wakefield, England

Elizabeth Cotton
Middlesex University Business School
Hendon, England
and
Founding Director of Surviving Work
www.survivingwork.org

CRC Press
Taylor & Francis Group
Boca Raton   London   New York

CRC Press is an imprint of the
Taylor & Francis Group, an **informa** business

CRC Press
Taylor & Francis Group
6000 Broken Sound Parkway NW, Suite 300
Boca Raton, FL 33487-2742

© 2019 by Taylor & Francis Group, LLC
CRC Press is an imprint of Taylor & Francis Group, an Informa business

No claim to original U.S. Government works

Printed on acid-free paper

International Standard Book Number-13: 978-1-1384-9796-2 (Paperback)
International Standard Book Number-13: 978-1-1384-9798-6 (Hardback)

Visit the Taylor & Francis Web site at
http://www.taylorandfrancis.com

and the CRC Press Web site at
http://www.crcpress.com

Contents

Foreword from first edition

Medical leadership means different things to different people in different contexts. Leaders exist because they have people following them who are able to see the vision and the courage that leaders bring with them. Sir John Tooke in his admirable report following the Medical Training Application Service (MTAS) debacle in England highlighted that one of the reasons for the crisis was a lack of medical leadership. Lord Darzi, the then health minister, also saw this as an important issue.

Are leaders born or made? How is leadership different from management? Who leads and why? What is management? What is administration? In secondary care settings the role of medical managers is crucial in setting the agendas for service planning, quality improvement and service delivery, ensuring that services remain patient-focused and patients and their families are satisfied with the services they receive. Leaders do the right thing in spite of challenges and they have the vision, courage and passion along with a style of communication that allows them to take people with them. Managers do things right, but the agenda may not be set by them. Medical leadership brings with it responsibility of improving clinical services, education, research and training. Medical leadership has many facets and skills.

This practical book is full of nuggets of wisdom of practical advice and theoretical underpinnings. I am sure medical professionals will find this of immense value and use in their day-to-day activities.

Dinesh Bhugra
Royal College of Psychiatrists

Foreword for the second edition

As doctors we are increasingly asked to take on leadership roles. Leadership is a skill most doctors possess – after all we lead in the hardest of all areas, the consulting room. As a general practitioner, there is nothing I have done in any leadership position that compares to my morning surgery. Working out which of the 30 or so patient encounters every day require further investigation, specialist input or active follow-up requires all the skills mentioned in *Practical Management and Leadership for Doctors*. We have to be decisive, organised, skilled communicators and deliver high-quality care – all in 10 minutes.

This is, of course, not to undermine the challenges of leading outside the consulting room and today many doctors do take on extended roles in a number of different settings. In fact, as the book points out, almost all senior doctors should be involved in management and leadership in some guise or other, if only to stop bad decisions being made and to influence the system to make it better for patients (Chapter 4). For those who enjoy leadership, the sky is the limit. During my career, I have held a number of national leadership positions, most notably as Chair of the Royal College of General Practitioners (2010–2013). Leading, whether in or out of the consulting room, is really about managing people, dealing with their expectations and fundamentally understanding that you get the most out of the teams or people you lead by modelling the behaviour you expect from them. I have written in the past about the leadership styles that you see in the current National Health Service (NHS) often exemplified by men – leading as if to battle, playing the 'heroic leader'. This contrasts with what I feel is most required, and the style I hope I have used most in my career – that is the 'Peloton Style', or dispersive leadership, whereby the workload of leadership is constantly being shared.

Whatever style one uses (and in fact, the most likely style is a mix depending on the needs of the day or organisational issue), *Practical Management and Leadership for Doctors* is a helpful guide. There must be thousands if not tens of thousands of books on leadership, yet this little tome stands out amongst the many aimed at doctors. Firstly, it is written for doctors, by those who understand how doctors think and work. Secondly, it is a useful tool for the busy, jobbing doctor to have to hand, with bite-size chapters, easily accessible help, case studies and summaries at the end of each chapter. Finally, the book is relevant to so many aspects of our working lives: It provides important and timely information on areas which we face every day such as managing change, running meetings and communicating effectively with staff; it talks to us about the pitfalls as well the joys of leading and how leadership is about engaging others; if we want people to listen to us, we must listen to them (Chapter 5, People skills).

The amount of jargon in the book is kept to a minimum and the references at the end of each chapter call us, if we want, to explore particular areas in more detail. The book draws on the work of the late Steven Covey and his *7 Habits of Highly Effective People*, and the two books should form part of most doctors' personal library on leadership. Perhaps my personal favourite is the final chapter, on Balance. For the last decade, I have been the doctor's doctor, seeing and treating doctors with mental health and/or addiction problems as part of the Practitioner Health Programme. Initially for doctors in the London area only, the service has since January 2017 been expanded across England to be available for all general practitioners.

Over the years, I have seen thousands of doctors with burnout, depression, anxiety – symptoms indistinguishable from post-traumatic stress disorder – as well as small numbers suffering from bipolar disorder and alcohol or drug addiction. Doctors go through the same difficulties as non-medical individuals (after all, we are not immune to loss, sickness, marital issues or other such traumatic life events). However, the biggest single cause of the mental illness amongst the doctors I see is their work, and in particular the demands placed on them through working in the modern, busy and demanding NHS. Doctors are trained to work hard and when the going gets tough, their natural inclination is to blame themselves and work harder. *Practical Management* tells us that 'your most important asset is yourself' and how it is all too common for people to succeed in their careers at the expense of a wrecked personal life. The authors warn us from suffering from 'superman or superwoman' syndrome and not to neglect our own humanity and health needs. Whilst we might need to give to others, we also should receive from them, maintaining 'the emotional credit line with our partners and others' described by Covey. The authors give us a simple exercise to perform, called the 'Self Factor'. This helps us identify our own needs – be they physical, psychological, creative or even spiritual – and how to use this information to prevent burnout and remain healthy in the workplace. I use a similar exercise amongst the doctors I see and it is helpful for this book on leadership to acknowledge the human limits of all leaders and not, as many books on leadership appear to do, perpetuate this myth of a super-person able to function always, anywhere and anyhow.

This book is light in weight, and heavy on common sense. It should form part of the doctor's armoury. Even those who do not see themselves as good leaders are often humble enough to be unaware of their potential leadership qualities.

I learnt from reading the book, and I am sure the reader will as well.

Clare Gerada

Preface

In the years that have elapsed since the first edition of this book, we have seen profound changes in healthcare and particularly in the National Health Service (NHS). Our choice of Gareth Morgan's metaphor of *organisation as flux and transformation* as one of the key concepts in Chapter 3 on understanding your organisation appears particularly prescient. At the core of the first edition was the importance of relationships to effective leadership and management, and that has not changed. However, there have been major changes in this edition throughout with the introduction of three new chapters. One of these focuses on innovation and change and examines how this can be led and managed using several practical examples. Another, also particularly apposite to the state of healthcare in many countries, and especially in the NHS, explores what to do as a leader and manager when the going gets tough. Finally, we have added a whole chapter on continuing professional development in management and leadership for doctors. It seems strange to realise that the joint Faculty of Medical Leadership and Management was only emerging as the first edition of this book was produced but now (alongside many other providers) has such an excellent range of educational and support programmes available.

We have also added another author to our team, Dr Elizabeth Cotton, who brings a particular interest in the stresses of working in healthcare settings as well as greater familiarity with primary care than the two original authors. We remain grateful to the panel of doctors – Professor Wendy Burn (now President of the Royal College of Psychiatrists) and Drs Suresh Chari, Kate Kucharska-Pietura, Ken McDonald and Jayanthi Devi Subramani – who read the drafts of the first edition, for their helpful comments and suggestions. To their number we now add Drs Aamer Sajjad and Gwenan Sykes, who have performed a similar service for the second edition. Whilst we are grateful to them, the responsibility for opinions expressed and any errors remains with the authors.

As before, as a practical book this edition is grounded in the experience of the authors in the English NHS, but we have designed the structure, examples, exercises and approach of the text in a way that we believe will find wide applicability. We have used illustrations from several different national contexts, particularly in the chapter on innovation and change. We believe this second edition updates and adds to the usefulness of the first.

John Wattis
Stephen Curran
Elizabeth Cotton

Authors

John Wattis is a Professor of Old Age Psychiatry, University of Huddersfield (UK). John was full-time Medical Director for Leeds Community and Mental Health NHS Trust from 1995 to 1999. He also held senior offices within the Faculty for Old Age Psychiatry of the Royal College of Psychiatrists. He has been research and development director for several National Health Service (NHS) trusts. Before his retirement from his consultant post in the NHS, he trained as a business and life coach. Since then he has continued in his visiting university post, lecturing various student groups and supporting research. He has taught basic and advanced coaching skills to psychiatrists through the Royal College of Psychiatrists Education and Training Centre and coached several NHS, university and voluntary sector staff, mostly in senior management positions. He has also acted for several years as part-time medical director (mental health) to two primary care trusts and continues to give medical management support on an *ad hoc* basis to these trusts.

Stephen Curran is a Professor of Old Age Psychiatry, University of Huddersfield (UK) and Consultant in Old Age Psychiatry, South West Yorkshire Partnership NHS Foundation Trust, Wakefield. Stephen trained in Leeds and worked as Lecturer in Old Age Psychiatry at the University of Leeds until he took up his current post as Consultant in Old Age Psychiatry in Wakefield in 1998. His primary clinical role is focused on acute in-patient service for older people, and he is also Lead Clinician for the Wakefield Memory Service. Since his appointment, Stephen has had several medical management roles including Programme Director, Head of Service and Clinical Lead. Since October 2017, he has been the Associate Medical Director for Postgraduate Medical Education. Stephen has contributed to significant changes in the organisation including service development and changes to the medical management arrangements. He also has considerable practical experience of dealing with the many management issues that arise in a busy old age psychiatry service including job planning, appraisal, quality improvements, change management and dealing with complaints, conflicts and the pressures caused by limited resources.

Elizabeth Cotton is a writer and educator working in the field of mental health at work. Her background is in workers' education and international development. She has worked in over 35 countries on diverse issues such as HIV/AIDS, organising and building grassroots networks, negotiating and bargaining with employers as head of education for Industrial, one of the largest trade unions in the world, reflected in her 2011 book, *Global Unions, Global Business* (Libri Publishers). She teaches and writes academically at Middlesex University about employment relations and precarious work. She is Editor-in-Chief of a UK Association of Business Schools journal, *Work, Employment and Society,* looking at the sociology of work. She blogs as www.survivingwork.org to a network of 30,000 people. In 2017, she published the largest national survey about working conditions in mental health, www.thefutureoftherapy.org. She set up www.survivingworkinhealth.org as a free resource in partnership with the Tavistock and Portman NHS Foundation Trust. Her current book, *Surviving Work in Healthcare: Helpful stuff for people on the frontline* (Gower, 2017), was nominated for the Chartered Management Institute's practitioner book of the year.

Introduction

DEVELOPING MANAGEMENT AND LEADERSHIP SKILLS

This book aims to be a practical introduction to the topic of medical management. Our purpose in writing this is to provide an easy-to-use guide for doctors in any kind of management role, including those preparing for their first
consultant or general practice principal post. We also want to help those moving
into more senior medical management posts to take stock and apply their knowledge and skills in a new setting. Our approach is rooted in our experience in
various clinical, academic and management posts in the National Health Service
(NHS) and universities. However, in view of the constant change in this and
other health systems, we have sought to keep the text open to wide application.
We have also been selective in our reference to the ever-developing management
literature, aiming for approaches that we know from experience work in practice.
Because this is a practical guide, we have included examples and exercises to support readers in applying the knowledge and skills covered to their own situation.
Hopefully readers will not only increase their competence as managers, they will
also increase their enjoyment.

Understanding the differences between administration, management and leadership

The distinction between administration, management and leadership is a vital
starting point (Box 1.1). Confusion between them leads to wasted time and even
to conflict.

Good *administration* is doing routine tasks well. A bureaucratic approach
works well here (see the section on *management cultures and cultural appropriateness* in Chapter 3). *Management* involves making things happen even when

---

> ## BOX 1.1: The distinction between administration, management and leadership
>
> *Administration*: Doing routine tasks well
> *Management*: Making things happen (often complex things in complex
>   environments)
> *Leadership*: Developing shared vision and direction towards a common
>   goal or purpose and getting the best out of people in serving that
>   purpose

the environment is not simple and the tasks themselves may be complicated. It requires attention to detail and often involves teamwork. *Leadership* means helping a group or organisation to find its direction and drawing the best out of people to serve a common purpose. Leadership motivates teams to work well.

Good administration is essential, but nobody should employ an expensive doctor to do simple, straightforward administrative tasks. On occasion, we still hear of doctors doing their own typing or filing for lack of adequate secretarial support. There is no problem in this for those doctors who have excellent keyboard skills and are supported by effective software and computer systems. However, too often doctors who do not have these skills are expected to act as typists when this is not a 'core skill'. Lack of adequate computer systems, software and support result in the wastage of many hours of expensive medical time. This can mean doctors working unpaid overtime and/or employers wasting medical competences and using doctors inefficiently. In addition, clinical records are now predominantly electronic and system failures can create significant clinical risks.

Modern medical practice is largely delivered by teamwork and so any consultant or principal in general practice will need at least a basic level of competency in management and leadership skills. Many newly appointed consultants and principals in general practice feel they have not acquired this basic level of competency through their training, which has understandably been focused on producing *competent clinicians*.

Those aspiring to more senior management roles as Clinical Directors, Medical Directors, Associate Medical Directors and to managerial roles in medical education will require much more than basic competency. Until recently, the development of higher levels of competency in these areas has been on an *ad hoc* basis although, historically, the British Association of Medical Managers developed its own 'Fit to Lead' programme with associated standards and competences. These covered the following areas:

- Communication
- Developing people
- Developing the business
- Developing self
- The wider contexts
- Quality

The Faculty of Medical Leadership and Management (FMLM) courses and programmes cover similar topics (https://www.fmlm.ac.uk). These competences are also covered in this book. The role of the FMLM in training and development is discussed in Chapter 10.

Doctors in senior management positions (such as Medical Directors), most of whom choose to continue in clinical practice, have the unenviable task of keeping up to date in both management and in their chosen area of clinical practice. Generally, continued involvement in clinical work by doctors in senior management roles helps them to keep in touch *and be seen to keep in touch* with clinical reality (see Chapter 5). There is enormous value in senior practising clinicians being involved in management, medical education and professional leadership. In senior medical management positions, the art is to design any involvement in clinical work, with the help of colleagues, in such a way that it is circumscribed so that interference in either direction between different roles is minimised. 'Protected time' for both clinical and management roles is vital and should be recognised as such by employers.

Leadership and management *can* be distinguished, but the relationship between them in successful organisations is close. Leadership defines direction, enables, empowers and even inspires, but without management competency, *it does not deliver.* The words we use to define management roles for doctors in the NHS demonstrate the complex interactions between 'direction', leadership and management:

- Medical Director (usually an *executive* director post)
- Associate Medical Director
- Clinical Director (often providing a lead and supported by a manager)
- Clinical Lead (not the same as clinical director or clinical leader)
- Team Leader (sometimes the team 'manager' rather than the leader)

Virtually all medical managers need also to be good leaders. But they have to work within a context of direction set by their organisation, and that can sometimes cause conflict.

Clarity about roles and what titles mean is important. If a service has a clinical *lead* and a non-medical *manager,* who defines the *direction?* (See Box 1.2.)

BOX 1.2: Conflict between management and leadership due to lack of clarity

A new specialist service is set up. A service manager is appointed, but the job description contains no reference to the relationship with the 'Clinical Lead'. The doctor appointed to Clinical Lead is unsure of his or her relationship to the manager. Normally, leadership sets the direction and management achieves the desired outcomes. Here it is different. The manager is heavily 'performance managed' (from earlier) according to national and locally determined 'targets'. So what is the role of the Clinical Lead? At one extreme, it could simply be to 'advise' the manager about clinical issues (so why not 'Clinical Advisor'?) or to 'lead' the clinical aspects of the service along a direction determined by others; at the other, it could be to innovate and inspire and give direction to the manager and the team. This can only be resolved by careful negotiation and explicit agreement between the manager and the Clinical Lead. This will need to involve more senior management and take into account the views of other members of the team. Failure to resolve this and to define the roles will lead to conflict and inefficiency.

EXERCISE 1.1
Different components of your job

Using three columns, make a list of the administrative, management and leadership components of your ('management') job. Eliminate any tasks in the administrative column (as far as possible) by delegation to others (secretary, management assistant, personnel officer and so on) and/or by using alternatives to traditional administrative support such as digital dictation. If you have nobody appropriate to delegate to, ask how and when such support can be developed and make it a priority. Now look at the largely leadership and management tasks that remain and put them into priority order. Decide how and when you will make time for the priority tasks. The rationale for this can be seen in Stephen Covey's bestselling management book, *The 7 Habits of Highly Effective People* [1].

This task has elements of the first three habits: being proactive, beginning with the end in mind and putting first things first.

CORE COMPETENCES OF MANAGERS AND LEADERS

Table 1.1 gives a list of some of the skills or competences that medical managers and leaders need (a couple of rows are blank for you to add your own ideas). This is not to suggest that the two roles are completely separate or that leaders do not need management skills and *vice versa* but to give a general idea of the different priorities of the two roles.

Table 1.1 Some competences of managers and leaders

Management	Leadership
Negotiation	Setting direction
Change management	Enabling
Supervision	Empowering
Conflict resolution	Involving
Delegation	Inspiring
Communicating information	Listening
Giving feedback	Influencing
Dealing with crises	Avoiding crises
Performance management	Leading by example

The trainee in medicine will have experience in a number of these skills. What doctor, in a modern health service, has not had to negotiate with patients and carers over treatment plans or with colleagues over on-call or leave arrangements? We have all seen change managed (almost constantly in the modern NHS, and not always well). All doctors in training should have had clinical and educational supervision. They will almost certainly have been involved in conflict resolution and crisis management and will have been the object of much delegation! They may not have had so much experience in setting direction; however, if they have been lucky in their training experience, they will have been supervised by consultants who were enabling, empowering, involving and even inspiring. Inevitably they will have been influenced by the examples (though not always good) of those with whom they have trained.

Many new consultants will feel that they have not had enough systematic teaching or practical experience in these areas, though this, like the support for those taking more senior management roles, is improving.

EXERCISE 1.2
Leadership and management competences

In two columns (one for management and one for leadership), make a list of the competences you believe you require for management and leadership in your current role. Rate yourself on a scale of 1 (poor) to 5 (excellent) in each competency. If you have trusted colleagues, you may wish to ask one or more of them to rate you too, to get different perspectives. Consider how you can make the most of the areas you are rated highly on and determine how important it is to improve any other areas. If it is important, make a time-limited plan to do something about these areas.

Achievement demands synergy between leadership and management. Staff working in the NHS often complain that 'paperwork and form filling' gets in the way of delivering good patient care. The following documented example illustrates that this frustration is a longstanding issue and not only confined to the health-care sector. The Duke of Wellington was a great military leader, but historians attribute some of his success to attention to detail in managing the logistics of his military operations. Inspired decisions on the battlefield were supported by months of careful preparation, despite the *administrative* tasks imposed by the central bureaucracy against which he sometimes rebelled (Box 1.3).

BOX 1.3: Duke of Wellington's dispatch to Whitehall (displayed at Mirehouse, the country home of one of his descendants in Cumbria)

August 1812
Gentlemen,

Whilst marching from Portugal to a position that commands the approach to Madrid and the French forces, my officers have been diligently complying with your requests, which have been sent by H. M. ship from London to Lisbon and thence by dispatch rider to our headquarters.

We have enumerated our saddles, bridles, tents and tent poles, and all manner of sundry items for which His Majesty's Government, holds me accountable. I have dispatched reports on the character, wit and spleen of every officer. Each item and every farthing has been accounted for, with two regrettable exceptions for which I beg your indulgence.

Unfortunately, the sum of one shilling and ninepence remains unac-counted for in one infantry battalion's petty cash and there has been hideous confusion as to the number of jars of raspberry jam issued to one cavalry regiment during a sandstorm in western Spain. This reprehensible carelessness may be related to the pressure of circumstances, since we are at war with France, a fact which may come as a bit of a surprise to you gentlemen in Whitehall.

This brings me to my present purpose, which is to request elucidation of my instructions from His Majesty's Government so that I may better understand why I am dragging an army over these barren plains. I con-strue that perforce it must be one of two alternative duties, as given in the following. I shall pursue either one with my best ability, but I cannot do both.

1. To train an army of uniformed British clerks in Spain for the benefit of the accountants and copy-boys in London, or, perchance.
2. To see to it that the forces of Napoleon are driven out of Spain.

Your most obedient servant,
Wellington.

STARTING IN A NEW SITUATION

In any new situation, whether on first appointment as a consultant, a principal in general practice, or as a medical manager of whatever grade, it is essential to start well. Handling the transition to a role with increased responsibilities is never easy, and it is always useful to make time to reflect on developing roles and responsibilities, preferably with the help of a mentor, coach or other level-headed person. Even if you have been in your current situation for some time, it makes sense to reappraise the situation and to make a fresh start from time to time. Often this needs to be done after at least a few months spent exploring the demands and limits of the role. The areas to be appraised to achieve this fresh start can be summed up in the 'three Rs', as follows:

- Roles
- Relationships
- Responsibilities

Roles

One of the strengths of how medicine is organised is that management jobs often involve continuing clinical practice (and sometimes academic and/or training roles as well). It is useful to make an inventory of key roles. See Table 1.2 for an example of key roles for a newly appointed Medical Director. Clarity about the key roles as they develop helps to ensure that no one area is neglected or sacrificed accidentally. It also enables a continuing review of both the roles and the priority to be given to them. One of the authors has even, from time to time, colour-shaded his weekly programme according to the different roles over a period of a week to get a clearer idea of which roles were taking the time! Be aware, if you do this, that one of the things you may find is that roles (especially administrative roles) that are not properly your own can be stealing time and that delegation is called for.

Organisations that are run by 'Boards', like NHS Trusts, have a mixture of Executive Directors in roles such as Chief Executive, Medical Director, Finance Director, Human Resources Director and Director of Quality supported by Non-Executive Directors chosen for their expertise in areas like accountancy, business management, local politics and so on. One of the Non-Executives acts as Chair of the Board and, collectively, they are responsible for providing a degree of outside scrutiny, support and common sense to guide the Executive Directors in their work and the Board in its decision-making. Once decisions are made, the Board is expected to stand behind them.

Figure 1.1 gives an example of how a 'balance wheel' can be used to look at the different roles, for example, of a newly appointed Medical Director and how well they are being fulfilled. In this kind of a plot, the subject makes a judgement about how well she or he is fulfilling each role on a scale of 0 (centre of circle) to 10 (periphery). Some people join the dots and make the point that if you end up with an odd shaped figure you are in for a 'bumpy ride'!

Table 1.2 Key roles for a newly appointed Medical Director

Role	Remarks
Medical advice and leadership to Board	This will involve good communication with relevant medical colleagues and fair evaluation of sometimes competing priorities. It will also involve good relationships with other Directors and a recognition of what they contribute.
Medical standards (including role as Responsible Officer [RO] for GMC revalidation), employment and disciplinary matters	Here the relationship with the Director of Human Resources, other human resources staff, the local representatives of the BMA and the doctor's own defence union as well as the GMC for issues of revalidation are likely to be helpful.
Leader of team of doctors	Mutual respect between members of the medical management team and senior colleagues is vital.
Continuing clinical work	For more junior management posts, clinical workload may only require minor adjustment; for the most-senior posts, it may have to be severely limited. In either case, smooth organisation and the co-operation of colleagues are essential.
Wider responsibilities	Some medical managers will also have roles within professional organisations of clinicians or of managers or be involved in wider health service or related work.
Other roles	At this stage, it does no harm to remind oneself of the wider roles within work (eg teacher, researcher) and outside of work (eg parent, partner, participator in recreational activities).

In this example there are eight radii, but there can be as many or as few as the situation demands. The labels applied to each radius here are roughly the same as in Table 1.2, but note that the issues of medical employment and standards (including Responsible Officer [RO] role) have been separated out in the table.

This tool can lead to a reappraisal of priorities. For example, the balance wheel above leads to an understanding that the issue of medical advice to the Board needs urgent action. Recruitment and retention of senior medical staff and leading the team of medical managers also appear to be priorities. Review of all the information in the balance wheel might lead to an action plan such as that outlined in Table 1.3.

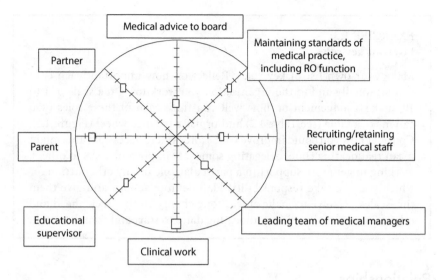

Figure 1.1 'Balance wheel' for the role of Medical Director.

Table 1.3 Illustrative action plan that might arise from considering the issues highlighted by the 'balance wheel' of Figure 1.1

Role	Action	Timing
Medical advice to Board	Discuss with Chief Executive.	Today
Recruiting/retaining senior medical staff	Discuss with Associate Medical Directors.	Next week
Maintaining standards of medical practice (including RO role)	Discuss (and if necessary, develop) policies with other relevant Directors. Find out more about the RO role in revalidation.	Before 'away day' below
Leading team of medical managers	Plan for 'away day' to develop shared vision and values.	Plan now for next month
Clinical work	No action.	
Educational supervisor	Explore support to trainee from another appropriate consultant.	This week
Parent	Get home on time.	Tonight
Partner	Don't neglect.	Always

EXERCISE 1.3
List your key roles

Make your own list of key roles. Reflect on how important each is to you personally and to the organisation you work for. On a scale of 1 to 10, make a judgement on how well you fulfil each of these roles (you can make a table (see Table 1.2) and/or use a balance wheel (Figure 1.1). Consider how you could improve your scores where necessary. This might mean reallocating time, delegating some less important tasks to others, working to get more support in a particular role or any other action for which you can take responsibility. Plan definite actions and give them timescales. Resolve to make at least one change in the week ahead and others incrementally, ideally allocating dates to start and complete each.

Relationships

Each of the earlier roles involves key relationships. Modern medicine is a team effort and good relationships are the foundation for effective clinical and managerial teams. Many failures in health and social services are blamed on poor communication; however, as the management writer Stephen Covey points out [1], good communication depends on trust and trust, in turn, is based on our assessment of the other person's 'character and competence'. This can be briefly expressed as a management 'equation':

$$\text{Communication} \sim \text{trust} = \text{character} \times \text{competence}$$

Starting in a new job, one needs to make a list (or 'mind map') of key relationships. These relationships will generally relate to the roles considered earlier. For example, in making sure adequate attention is paid to medical opinion on the board in the previous example, the Chief Executive is a key relationship. Other Directors with clinical responsibilities are also likely to be important in this context. In issues of medical staffing and discipline, the Personnel Director and any medical personnel specialist are likely to figure and so on.

What makes effective relationships at work? Here is a list that you may wish to expand:

- Mutual respect
- Shared vision (and mission)
- Shared values

- Clear definitions of roles and responsibilities
- Flexibility (within limits)
- Integrity

Mutual respect is a vital starting point, but how often do we hear doctors 'slagging off' managers or *vice versa?* Barack Obama, in his autobiographical treatise on reshaping American politics, *The Audacity of Hope* [2], stressed the importance of respecting the views of others even when we don't agree with them. This is especially important in the current UK context. People have very different views about a wide range of topics including Brexit, religion, immigration, privatisation of public services and political parties, and these diverse and often split political and ethical positions will also be reflected in the people we work with. As a foundation for effective team working, it's essential to acknowledge, accept and respect this diversity. This requires a degree of empathy, of willingness to see and acknowledge the other person's point of view. It requires spending time finding out about their values, their understanding of what motivates people and their vision for how services should run and be developed. It emphatically does not involve the lazy prejudice of always imputing the worst motives to others. We all need to understand and respect each other's positions. That is the starting point of good relationships.

Within the work context, *shared vision* is also crucial. This does not come naturally and requires hard work. It applies at all levels. The clinical team needs shared vision. The different elements of a service require shared vision. The different parts of an organisation need shared vision. At Board level this vision needs to be a guiding principle that is genuinely shared not only by board members but by all managers, clinicians and other employees. Everyone in the organisation should be able to articulate what the organisation is there for (mission), where it is heading (vision) and how it intends to get there (values). Lack of such shared understanding leads to inefficiency and disruption within any organisation as different factions pull in different directions. When an organisation is new, shared vision can be developed by a process that involves all staff and also takes fully into account the ideas of service users.

In practice, a strong vision for future direction often comes from a Chief Executive or senior manager. But, however charismatic the manager, it is essential to listen to other people's points of view and to ensure, as far as possible, that all staff feel genuine 'ownership' of the vision. A doctor newly appointed to a management position needs to find out what senior managers think about the purpose and direction of the organisation. He or she may even need to help others to become clear about this.

If *mission* is what we as an organisation are there for and *vision* is about the direction we are heading in, *values* are about how we get there. What standards of behaviour are expected of us? Values can be expressed in an ethical code. The General Medical Council's (GMC's) statement on 'Duties of a Doctor' [3] (Box 1.4) is at once an expression of standards and of their underpinning values.

BOX 1.4: Duties of a doctor

Patients must be able to trust doctors with their lives and health. To justify that trust, you must show respect for human life and you must do the following:

- Make the care of your patient your first concern.
- Protect and promote the health of patients and the public.
- Provide a good standard of practice and care.
- Keep your professional knowledge and skills up to date.
- Recognise and work within the limits of your competence.
- Work with colleagues in the ways that best serve patients' interests.
- Treat patients as individuals and respect their dignity.
- Treat patients politely and considerately.
- Respect patients' right to confidentiality.
- Work in partnership with patients.
- Listen to patients and respond to their concerns and preferences.
- Give patients the information they want or need in a way they can understand.
- Respect patients' right to reach decisions with you about their treatment and care.
- Support patients in caring for themselves to improve and maintain their health.
- Be honest and open and act with integrity.
- Act without delay if you have good reason to believe that you or a colleague may be putting patients at risk.
- Never discriminate unfairly against patients or colleagues.
- Never abuse your patients' trust in you or the public's trust in the profession.

You are personally accountable for your professional practice and must always be prepared to justify your decisions and actions.

Source: General Medical Council, Good medical practice, https://www.gmc-uk.org/ethical-guidance/ethical-guidance-for-doctors/good-medical-practice, 2013.

Though the GMC publishes more detailed guidance on management and leadership for doctors [4], this general ethical statement, with minor additions, serves as a statement of values for doctors involved in management. Some of the key duties of a doctor in the workplace are summarised in Box 1.5. It is worth emphasising that the delivery of good quality patient care can only be done if we respect each other as clinicians and work to build teams that can communicate effectively, even when there are disagreements.

BOX 1.5: Duties of a doctor in the workplace

Doctors make an important contribution to the management and leadership of health services and the delivery of healthcare. All doctors have some responsibility for using resources. Many will also lead teams or be involved in supervision of colleagues. Although the primary duty of doctors is for the care and safety of patients, whatever their role, doctors must do the following:

- Engage with colleagues to maintain and improve the safety and quality of patient care.
- Contribute to discussions and decisions about improving the quality of services and outcomes.
- Raise and act on concerns about patient safety.
- Demonstrate effective team working and leadership.
- Promote a working environment free from unfair discrimination, bullying and harassment, bearing in mind that colleagues and patients come from diverse backgrounds.
- Contribute to teaching and training doctors and other healthcare professionals, including by acting as a positive role model.
- Use resources efficiently for the benefit of patients and the public.
- The document also gives guidance on working with colleagues, maintaining and improving standards of care, recruitment, supervision, teaching, grievance procedures, performance and health related issues, using resources and writing references.

Source: General Medical Council, Leadership and management for all doctors, https://www.gmc-uk.org, 2012.

Putting the patient first and a wider concern for the health of the population are (or should be) what the NHS is all about. It is not just clinicians who have an obligation to provide a good standard of clinical practice and care. *Clinical governance* placed that obligation on all healthcare organisations. Apart from clinical standards, management practice, too, has its standards, expressed through the duties of *corporate governance*, which covers financial and other aspects of probity. Doctors who are managers, like other managers, need to keep up to date, to recognise their limits and to 'work in partnership with colleagues', co-operating in the interest of patients (and the wider population). In some cases, management concepts may be wider than clinical concepts. For example, management understanding of confidentiality may also embrace concepts such as commercial confidentiality or intellectual property rights. Listening, giving necessary information, respecting employees viewpoints (though not necessarily giving every employee the primacy the patient enjoys in the management of a medical condition) and supporting employees are all useful management values. Honesty and integrity speak for themselves.

So the ethical values of doctors and the ethical values of managers (at least in a public service organisation) can be easily aligned and compared. In commercial organisations, the duty to return a profit for shareholders can appear to be in conflict with some of the other duties. This is one of the reasons that some people have reservations about the introduction of more 'for-profit' companies into the provision of NHS services. Clarity is essential in this situation. In medical ethics, the other values of a healthcare organisation are equally as important as (and, in the case of 'putting patients first', more important than) 'duty to shareholders'.

Clear definitions of roles and responsibilities enable people to work efficiently and effectively without constantly 'tripping over' invisible boundaries (see Box 1.2). It is remarkable how often, in a complicated organisation like the NHS, definitions are unclear. This can result in much wasted effort and sometimes in bad feelings.

Flexibility (within limits) is just as important as clear boundaries. Sometimes we may choose to take on extra work outside of our normal duties. However, we should always beware of unlimited flexibility resulting in overwork or lack of clear definition or of flexibility that, ratchet-like, only works in one direction.

Integrity in the sense of being true to oneself and fair to others is an essential factor in successful management and leadership. Machiavelli's ideas notwithstanding, people work better when they know they can trust their colleagues. The multiple roles of medical managers make integrity particularly important. Great clarity of thinking and boundary-setting are needed to maintain integrity (see Box 1.6).

Responsibilities

Doctors were historically trained to have a clear sense of personal responsibility for patients under their care, though fragmentation of care by increasing specialisation and industrialisation of services has somewhat eroded this in many areas of practice. Consultants generally feel that they have the authority (though not always the resources) in the clinical situation to discharge their clinical responsibilities. Even in the clinical situation, in complex areas like psychiatry, responsibility may be shared (again, the GMC [5] has a document). However, responsibility should never be so diffuse that nobody takes it! Responsibility for ensuring the care or treatment plan is delivered may rest with the care coordinator or the case manager, and it is essential that employers take responsibility for ensuring that clinicians of all disciplines have the necessary competences to undertake tasks that they are expected to perform. Traditionally the GMC has laid on doctors the duty to ensure that anybody to whom they delegate care is competent to deliver that care. In a large multidisciplinary team, this responsibility now rests with the employer. However, if doctors have doubts about the competency of colleagues, they are expected to act.

How, exactly, to act will depend on circumstances. It may involve talking to the colleague face to face. If the colleague is from another discipline and the matter

---

BOX 1.6: Maintaining integrity

After a meeting, a consultant 'buttonholes' the Medical Director and asks for 'a quiet word'. The Medical Director takes the colleague (Dr A), who is clearly angry, to a private office. The consultant asks if he can speak about a colleague (Dr B) 'in confidence'. The Medical Director (who has been in similar situations before) reminds his colleague that confidentiality is always bounded. If he hears about anything where his duties as a doctor or as a manager require him to act, he will not be able to guarantee confidentiality. The colleague accepts this and, before the Medical Director can say more, launches into an account of his fury that Dr B has sent him an email concerning leave arrangements that he considers to be demeaning and bullying. Dr B has compounded this 'offence' by copying the email to a several colleagues.

What happens next will depend on circumstances. If this is the first time the Medical Director has heard of Dr B behaving in this way, she might adopt a coaching or mentoring approach to help Dr A to find a way of dealing with Dr B (with or without any intervention from the Medical Director). If this is not the first time that such issues have surfaced and previous informal attempts to resolve them have failed, or if the email is so outrageous as to demand further action, the Medical Director needs to decide whether a more formal investigation and intervention is required. If this is the case, the Medical Director has maintained her integrity by reminding Dr A that confidentiality is always bounded.

---

is of serious concern, it may necessitate talking to a service manager, Clinical Director or a manager in that particular discipline. Doctors should always have a mentor or other trusted peer to whom they can go for support in deciding what to do if they have concerns of this nature. Ultimately, they should be able to consult a medical manager and/or their defence organisation for support and advice. The best course of action will depend on local structures and relationships as well as upon the nature and severity of the concern. Nobody should feel alone in dealing with this kind of situation. If they do, management has failed.

When we move away from the clinical situation to the managerial situation, responsibilities, boundaries and authority are often hard to pin down. Nevertheless, it is worth the effort to obtain clarity.

To roles, responsibilities and relationships we could add a fourth 'R' – *resources*. There rarely seem to be enough to do the job as well as the well-trained professional wants. For the medical manager there is a twofold duty. First, it is imperative to make the best possible use of available resources (*efficiency*). Second, where a case can be made for extra resources, it is important to prioritise need and to make an evidence-based 'business case' for the development or re-allocation of resources (*equity*). Simply complaining that there is not enough is inadequate.

CONCLUSIONS

In this chapter we have considered the distinctions between administration, management and leadership. We have begun to look at the competences needed to manage and lead successfully. We have suggested a framework for evaluating the roles, relationships and responsibilities of the managerial component of any medical job. In doing this we have emphasised the complexity of the roles undertaken by medical managers and the necessity for good working relationships. In the next chapter we will look more closely at key relationships and how to keep them healthy. Later chapters will examine the impact of different management cultures and the need to be able to operate efficiently in the various cultures found in any large organisation. We will examine some of the key skills and competences that medical managers need to develop. We will look at developing and sharing personal vision and values and at maintaining personal (including 'work–life') balance. We will examine the importance of 'iteration' in developing understanding for senior managers. Co-operative ways of working and thriving in an ever-changing environment are also highlighted. Our last chapters revisit some of the earlier work on personal balance and seek to support medical managers in keeping going and knowing when to stop!

REFERENCES

1. Covey SR (2016) *The 7 Habits of Highly Effective People*. FranklinCovey, Mango Media Inc. (Kindle Edition).
2. Obama B (2008) *The Audacity of Hope*. Edinburgh, UK: Canongate.
3. General Medical Council (2013a) Good medical practice. https://www.gmc-uk .org/guidance/good_medical_practice.asp.
4. General Medical Council (2012) Leadership and management for all doctors. https://www.gmc-uk.org.
5. General Medical Council (2013b) Accountability in multi-disciplinary and multi-agency mental health teams. https://www.gmc-uk.org/static /documents/content/Accountability_in_multi-disciplinary_and _multi-agency_mental_health_teams.pdf.

2

Maintaining productive key relationships

No man is an island...

John Donne (1572–1631)

In the current healthcare climate, the space to establish good working relationships is not built into our day. Many workplace cultures have become so focused on delivering targets and fire-fighting that we are often operating within environments where conflict and miscommunication between staff is common. The Francis inquiries are stark warnings not to underestimate the anti-relational factors at play within the NHS including cultures of blame, bullying and racism. These are realities that we must be aware of in order to successfully relate to the people we work with. This chapter aims to encourage you to put the work of building relationships with colleagues at the centre. The proposal is for us to try to understand the complex relationships that we have to manage at work and the need to devote thought and time in building collegial relationships with the people we work with.

UNDERSTANDING OUR INTERACTIONS WITH COLLEAGUES

Medical school selection procedures mean that doctors are usually very intelligent in the sense that they are intellectually bright and academically accomplished. However, research on so-called emotional intelligence (EI) shows that in many areas EI is a stronger predictor of success than intellect [1]. There are many definitions of EI and, unlike conventional intelligence, it is said to be relatively easy to develop. It can be characterised as competency in interpersonal interaction based on empathy, self-awareness, self-regulation, self-motivation, social awareness, and social skills. There are many questionnaires designed to measure EI or 'emotional quotient' (EQ), somewhat analogous to intelligence quotient (IQ). Despite the fact that (rather like IQ) it is a concept with disputed boundaries and properties, it nonetheless describes something that is pragmatically useful in understanding management issues.

Transactional analysis (TA) [2] is another useful framework for looking at interactions. It is represented in Figure 2.1. Like EI theory, TA recognises that we are not strictly rational beings who relate to each other in patterns determined entirely by logic. It recognises that when we interact with others we do so in ways that are as much determined by emotions and past experience as by the present facts. Like other conceptual frameworks we will use (eg organisational culture in the next chapter), TA is essentially metaphorical in nature and, as such, subject to many limitations [3]. Nevertheless, it is a useful tool for understanding and managing our relationships on a day-to-day basis. In essence, it asserts that we all have three main ego states from which we can interact with others. The parent state (P) has two 'supervisory' functions. One incorporates the nurturing side of parenthood, the other (critical parent) the 'oughts' and 'shoulds' we internalise as we grow up. Some of these may be very useful and some may be distinctly unhelpful. In this metaphor, the adult ego state (A) sees, hears, thinks and comes up with reality-based solutions to problems. The child ego state (C) is more emotional and carries emotional memories from childhood. When it is 'hooked', sometimes by the perceived 'parental' communication of a colleague, childhood emotions inappropriate to the present situation can come rushing to the fore. Like the parent function, it has two subdivisions: the 'compliant' and the 'rebellious' child. Two other concepts from TA are useful in understanding the social psychology of human interaction. One is the idea of 'crossed' transactions, when, for example, one person communicates on an A–A level, but the other perceives the comment as critical and responds with a C–P communication. An example might be 'How long have we got to discuss this situation?' (A–A) with the response 'Why are you always rushing me?' (C–P). The other useful idea is that we all have 'scripts', which are learned ways of dealing with situations. Again,

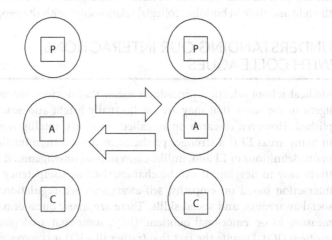

Figure 2.1 Parent (P), adult (A) and child (C) ego states as envisaged in TA: A–A transaction illustrated.

these are sometimes useful, sometimes not and, even when useful, may impede our flexibility. An excellent brief introduction to TA has been written by [4].

Of course, there are many other ways of looking at the psychodynamics of dyadic and group relationships, but we will focus on these two which incorporate the understanding that we are not completely rational beings. Equipped with these tools, let us look at some of the key interactions of doctors in management roles.

RELATIONSHIPS IN THE MULTIDISCIPLINARY TEAM

A common scenario for doctors is entry into a multidisciplinary team as a consultant. This is often not a well-defined role and difficulties can easily arise. One of the commonest causes of difficulty is different expectations (see Box 2.1).

BOX 2.1: A case of different expectations

A doctor is appointed to replace a consultant colleague who has just retired early. The new consultant has a consensual style of leadership. He shares the ward with another consultant who is more authoritarian. He finds that ward staff are constantly asking his secretary to fix appointments for him to speak to patients' relatives. On a number of occasions relatives are somewhat apologetic, explaining that they only wanted a 'progress report' and didn't need to 'bother' the consultant. Looking at his ever–more crammed schedule, the doctor decides that he needs to develop a 'screening' system so that when relatives ask for information, they get it from the primary nurse or the ward doctor in the first instance and are only referred to the consultant if the issue is particularly difficult. The doctor decides to discuss his ideas first with the more experienced colleague. The colleague explains that she has tried to implement such a system for the last 5 years without success. Nurses have always resisted her plans for them to deal with things directly, but she is willing to back up her new colleague if he wants to 'have a go'. The new consultant makes an appointment to talk to the senior ward manager. He lays before her the issue of his diary not having enough space to see so many relatives and asks if she has any ideas to support him in dealing with the issue. She says that his predecessor always wanted to see relatives personally and did not trust nurses to 'give out information'. He tries again, asking what the ward manager thinks. She says the other consultant on the ward would need to agree to any change in 'policy'. The new consultant says he thinks he can deliver that and proposes a 'triage' system where the appropriate nurse from the primary nursing team takes all queries from relatives and decides whether to deal with them by herself, to deal with them jointly with the junior doctor or to refer to the consultant. There is always the option to involve the consultant if necessary. After further negotiation and some training for the staff, this scheme is successfully implemented (and the consultant's schedule is less crowded).

The previous example can be understood using concepts from both EI and TA. The EI of the new consultant is demonstrated in several ways. He does not react to the situation by raving about the impossibility of fitting so much into his diary but looks for the causes of the situation. Once he has understood the source of the problem, he considers possible options but then realises he does not want to go ahead without understanding the position of his senior colleague. Having done this, he approaches the ward manager in what in TA terms is an 'adult–adult' communication. She does not respond directly to his approach but reacts in what is essentially a 'child–parent' way. He does not allow himself to be 'hooked' into criticising his retired colleague, nor does he snap back 'Well, I'm different' but asks again for her thoughts. Again, she responds defensively but, because he has prepared well, he is able to reassure her and propose a clear way of dealing with the situation. It is not put into effect immediately (culture change is rarely rapid), but after further negotiation and training the proposal is implemented successfully.

Another insight from TA is useful here. It is not only individuals who have 'scripts' (habitual ways of dealing with things based on past experience), organisations also tend to deal with things in the way they have always done. Different professions also may typically have different perspectives on how the multidisciplinary team works. Some of these are *stereotypes* and need to be shifted if genuine co-operation is to flourish.

At a lecture reporting a study on multidisciplinary working in forensic psychiatry, an academic from a nursing background suggested to the speaker that the problems were all due to the behaviour of doctors and the medical model. The sociologist who was giving the lecture refused to affirm this prejudice. It is important to bring any maladaptive beliefs about authority and responsibility in the team into the open in a way that encourages respectful adult–adult communication and resolution. Unless we agree about our purpose, vision and values, we are unlikely to function well together. It is a function of leadership to facilitate this agreement. Interestingly, management research shows that 'followers' put *trust, compassion, stability and hope* ahead of vision as qualities they wanted in leaders [5]. Trust and compassion are clearly functions of good (emotionally intelligent, adult–adult) relationships.

EXERCISE 2.1
Team working

(If you don't work in a multidisciplinary clinical or management team or you work in one where everyone always works well together, you can skip this one.)

Look at the team you work in and select an area where there seems to be misunderstandings between yourself and other team members. Seek to understand their position and where it originates. (You may need to listen to them to achieve this!) See whether you can jointly understand the source of the problems and find some solutions (you may need to involve others). Agree on a plan to implement the solutions, and on how you will all know you have succeeded. Agree a time to review progress.

We are not suggesting that all problems can always be solved by an individual taking action. In fact, in a complicated organisation, individuals often need to enlist others if they are going to make a real and lasting difference. For further details on approaches to this, see Chapter 8, especially the section on change management.

Sometimes, the co-operative approach may not work with an individual or group from a different discipline. If there are important differences that cannot be resolved on an informal face-to-face basis, one has to consider the other options. These should generally be discussed with a respected and experienced colleague. They may involve working with an individual's line manager, or seeking sponsorship for developmental work with the other person or the group, led by an appropriately skilled facilitator. One thing is certain, if an important relationship within the clinical (or management) team is dysfunctional, it does not pay to ignore it. If we avoid the problem, we may allow it to become worse (and harder to deal with when we can avoid it no longer).

So far, we have looked at how we deal with problems. We can reduce the frequency of problems by adhering to the principles of good relationships outlined in Chapter 1:

- Mutual respect
- Shared vision (and mission)
- Shared values
- Clear definitions of roles and responsibilities
- Flexibility (within limits)
- Integrity

It pays to build good relationships. In the context of family relationships, [6] writes of 'building the emotional bank account'. Reference [7] devotes a whole chapter of his book on Leadership in the context of the Virginia Mason Production System, discussed in Chapter 8, to the essential need for *respect* for people. *Genuine* interest in others and their points of view, acknowledgement of their skills and competences and a respectful attitude where there is genuine disagreement will do a lot to build team cohesion. Some of the approaches used in coaching (see Chapters 5 and 11) are helpful here.

RELATIONSHIPS WITH DOCTORS

There are many different kinds of working relationships between doctors (this list aims to be illustrative rather than exhaustive):

- Master–apprentice
- Educational supervisor/clinical supervisor–student/trainee
- Peer relationships (eg between a group of primary care doctors and/or consultants)
- Clinical Director–specialist consultant–specialty doctor
- Medical Director–Clinical Director–consultant

We have put 'master–apprentice' first because medicine is an ancient profession and (certainly up until recently) there have been strong elements of the old 'master–apprentice' relationship in training. The idea of consultant or principal in primary care medicine as 'master' of his or her craft is still present and explains the way in which consultants and principals in general practice still sometimes tend to regard themselves as independent 'craftsmen'. The 'apprenticeship' model is still often used to apply to learning in the clinical situation. Now is not the place to go into the attitudes and practices (some helpful, some not) that still survive from the 'master–apprentice' era. However, it is well to remember that this is still relatively recent history and still affects how people behave. There are also overlaps with the 'club' culture (the masters are all members of the 'club') and the 'craft' culture discussed in the next chapter.

SUPERVISORY AND EDUCATIONAL RELATIONSHIPS

Nobody now learns to be a doctor by staying with one master of a particular branch of the craft for many years. Instead we have a highly structured university curriculum for undergraduates and complicated training schemes for various 'specialties'. Most doctors, even in their training years, will have had some involvement with medical students. When they become consultants or principals in general practice, they will often take on a new role as educational or clinical supervisors of doctors in training. They will have had this role 'modelled' for them during their own training and, especially with recent changes in the format and assessment of postgraduate training, they are likely themselves to have had some special training for this role. Although not the only skill set needed for educational supervision, many of the skills used in coaching (Chapter 5) are relevant here (Box 2.2).

The educational supervisor and the clinical supervisor may be the same person but are now frequently separate, with the educational supervisor being responsible for several trainees. This has the advantage of improving standardisation and consistency of training. The advantage of the same person having both roles is that there is no disjunction between clinical and educational supervision. The potential disadvantage is that in the case of a personality clash or disagreement with the clinical supervisor, the trainee cannot turn to the educational supervisor. However, there is usually a College Tutor or scheme organiser who can fill this role. Broadly speaking, for most doctors, supervisory relationships have two main components. One is developmental (epitomised by coaching skills), the

---

BOX 2.2: Some definitions of terms used in educational supervision and training

Clinical supervisor: A trainer who is selected and appropriately trained to be responsible for overseeing a specified trainee's clinical work and providing constructive feedback during a training placement. Some training schemes appoint an educational supervisor for each placement. The roles of clinical and educational supervisor may then be merged.

Educational supervisor: A trainer who is selected and appropriately trained to be responsible for the overall supervision and management of a specified trainee's educational progress during a training placement or series of placements. The educational supervisor is responsible for the trainee's educational agreement.

other involves clinical supervision and, increasingly, assessment. There can be tensions between these roles but all are important. If the developmental role is handled skilfully, the supervisory role is usually less burdensome and assessment less threatening. We are responsible for our students and doctors in training, especially for ensuring we do not delegate to them tasks beyond their present competence. It scarcely seems possible that one of the authors did locums whilst still a medical student, when he was expected to help 'cover' casualty. Fortunately, we have moved on since then and the problems in training today tend to be in the opposite direction, with the need to make sure that trainees are sufficiently 'stretched' and gain sufficient breadth of supervised clinical experience gradually to develop sound independent clinical judgement.

The clinical and educational supervisors are also responsible for identifying issues of underperformance and dealing with them. The supervisor will generally do this with the support of the appropriate medical personnel/human resources department and in collaboration with a College Tutor, training-scheme organiser or another experienced colleague. Minor issues can be dealt with locally but if they cannot be resolved in a satisfactory way, then colleagues from the appropriate educational authority must become involved (see Box 2.3).

BOX 2.3: Helping a trainee with problems

Dr Jones had been appointed as a senior trainee in psychiatry. She had done well in her interview. No concerns were raised and her references were very good. The first year of her training was uneventful. During her second year of training, a number of minor issues were raised. She was arriving late at work more often and needed to be reminded about completing letters. There were also increasing errors on prescriptions, one resulting in a formal investigation by the pharmacy department when amoxycillin was prescribed to a patient allergic to penicillin. The clinical/educational supervisor had a meeting with Dr Jones, but no specific issues were identified. The problems continued and seemed to worsen, so after consultation Dr Jones agreed to meet the local College Tutor but again no progress was at first made in relation to trying to understand the underlying problem. After a number of meetings with the tutor, Dr Jones admitted that she didn't feel 'well' but didn't want to discuss it with local doctors because she was worried that she 'might lose her job'. She was encouraged to go and see her general practitioner (GP) but in addition an appointment was made for her to discuss her situation with the Training Programme Director for the scheme. The meeting proved very successful. Dr Jones explained that she had had a recent bereavement and was feeling low in mood but had felt concerned about discussing this with her consultant (who was both the clinical and educational supervisor) as she felt it might affect her future reference. She agreed to see her GP and her wish not to discuss this with local colleagues was respected.

In the UK, the 'specialty grade' doctor, incorporating the old staff grade and associate specialist grades, but also potentially allowing progression to admission to the specialist register, has made relationships more complicated. These doctors generally have not progressed far enough in training to be admitted to the specialist register and still work under the supervision of a consultant who is on the specialist register and retains a degree of responsibility for the clinical quality of their work. Consultants who have worked with high-quality staff grade and associate specialist colleagues will appreciate that a 'light touch' supervisory relationship can be very successful. However, some doctors in this grade expect to work too independently and may resent supervision. Issues of quality and clinical responsibility will have to be clearly negotiated and understood if this grade is to multiply (as envisaged by some NHS employers).

EXERCISE 2.2
Delegation in clinical practice

Before delegating a piece of work to a colleague in training, consultants need to consider the doctor's competences and what level of delegation is appropriate. They also need to be explicit about the level of delegation. For the task of reviewing a patient referred from a GP or hospital consultant, three possible levels of delegation are described in the following:

1. 'See the patient, make notes and discuss with me and see the patient together before deciding on and recording a management plan'.
2. 'See the patient, make notes, decide on and record a provisional diagnosis and management plan. Discuss with me (and see the patient together and/or make modifications to the plan if necessary) before it is implemented'.
3. 'See the patient, make notes, decide on and record a management plan. Only discuss with me immediately if you are uncertain or perceive a possible problem. Otherwise present the case briefly in routine clinical supervision'.

You may wish to modify these levels. When you are satisfied with them, consider what level(s) of delegation are appropriate to the doctors who work under your supervision as trainees or in 'staff' positions. Are you explicit about the level of delegation when you ask a doctor under your supervision to undertake an assessment or other clinical task? (What about delegation of management or administrative tasks to assistants or clerical staff? How do these principles apply in that situation?)

RELATIONSHIPS WITH MEDICAL 'PEERS'

Here we are, of course, not talking about relationships with colleagues (in the UK) who have been elevated to the House of Lords but with colleagues at an equivalent 'level' in their careers. When we are in training, our peers are our colleagues at the same stage in their training. When we become consultants or principals in general practice, other consultants and GPs are our peers. Because of the historical idea that once we are ready for 'independent' practice (on the specialist or GP register in modern parlance) we are all 'master craftsmen', the relationships between doctors in management and their consultant/principal colleagues (which will be discussed later) can also be viewed as peer relationships even though they may contain a managerial supervisory element.

'Independent practice' is an old-fashioned notion. 'Interdependence', within a regulatory framework, better describes the modern situation where technical advances have made it necessary that we trust and work closely with colleagues in other specialist areas. We all value highly a radiologist, haematologist, chemical pathologist or other colleague who provides timely and concise reports and advice on unusual findings or specialist colleagues who advise on a condition that may be commonplace to them but appears complicated and unusual to us!

High-quality relationships are essential between GPs and specialists in specialties dealing with chronic illnesses in the community rather than 'one-off' interventions in hospital. Doctors in permanent posts need to work to develop and sustain such relationships. Doctors in training or 'medical agency' posts may find this harder to do. One way of doing this for consultants is by going out and meeting GPs in local practices to seek their views on service provision and to seek opportunities for mutual learning. In theory, Care Commissioning Groups (CCGs) should have led to more dialogue between doctors in primary and secondary care. In practice, the CCGs have sometimes seemed remote and have not always led to better relationships. At the clinical level, a more formal but important way of working together is by developing 'shared care' protocols for common diseases and disorders. Finally, perhaps the most important way of working together is working together in the care of individual patients. This personal collaboration has become difficult with the development of ever–more fragmented patterns of care but it is important for patients and for doctors, especially in specialties like psychiatry where inpatient and community teams are often led by different consultants.

Within a specialty, peer groups can, through clinical audit, second opinions and confidential discussion of case management, provide a valuable space to reflect on and refine practice. This kind of case-based discussion is likely to become an increasingly important part of development for doctors in training and of appraisal for consultants. In any case, we would advocate consultants (and GPs) finding more time to discuss 'difficult cases' with their colleagues in addition to more structured clinical audit projects. Sustained effort is needed to maintain co-operative relationships. Competition of a friendly nature can be beneficial, but hostile competition makes for an unhappy workplace.

RELATIONSHIPS BETWEEN DOCTORS IN MANAGEMENT AND OTHER DOCTORS

The exercise of power is a delicate matter. The old 'merit award' system in the NHS used to give senior colleagues in hospital specialties an unspecified power in deciding who was 'meritorious' (and therefore who got significant supplements to their salaries). Now, Clinical Excellence Awards (CEAs) have replaced the merit award system and there are local CEA schemes and a national CEA scheme. Submissions to the local CEA scheme are reviewed by a panel, and consultants that are not applying for a CEA can apply to sit on the panel. All the arrangements for the local CEAs are reviewed and approved by the Local Negotiating Committee (where the management and staff side agree procedures). General experience is that this is a fair process. After awards have been made, all the submitted evidence and details of the awards are published, making the process transparent. Fears that the newer schemes would put too much power in the hands of medical managers and encourage division appear not to have been realised. We generally get the best out of people when we respect their abilities and (in the words of the former Chief Medical Officer, Liam Donaldson, when clinical governance was introduced) when we strive to 'create an environment in which clinical excellence can flourish' [8].

But we are getting ahead of ourselves. Consultant practice in the NHS has tended to be a very autonomous affair. In the heyday of the asylums, there had been doctors in charge ('medical superintendents'); but until the 1990s, the only doctors in formal management positions tended to be public health physicians with roles as area, district or regional medical officers. Consultants and GPs still tended to regard themselves as independent practitioners, answerable only to the General Medical Council (GMC). With the introduction of NHS Trusts, medical management became more formal. Every Trust was required to have a Medical Director, with Board-level responsibilities. In Hospital Trusts, they were often supported by consultant 'Clinical Directors' in specialties or clusters of specialties. Some mental health Trusts adopted a similar structure. Others had 'Associate Medical Directors' divided by specialty or, sometimes, by geographical area or other area of responsibility (eg Research and Development or Education).

Changes in the management of primary care have given many GPs more opportunity to be involved in management in England through CCGs and various posts in NHS England. Some GPs have also been involved in devising Sustainability and Transformation Plans (STPs) and are likely to be involved in their implementation through Accountable Care systems. How real this involvement is for the average

GP is questionable. Even those who are formally involved on steering groups may feel powerless in the light of financial constraints, top-down edicts and the advice of costly management consultants [9].

Massive and continuing organisational changes in the management of healthcare over the last 25 years in England (and elsewhere) have led to a need for doctors to receive more formal education in issues relating to management and leadership. This, together with issues relating to continuing professional development in this area, is discussed in Chapter 10.

The idea that the organisation and its Directors, including Medical Directors, were responsible not just for financial and corporate governance but also for the overall quality of clinical services attained prominence in England near the beginning of this period [8]. This and other pressures led to a demand for job planning, appraisal and eventually revalidation, recertification and relicensing of consultants and GPs. This meant that doctors in management had to take on new roles as *Responsible Officers* (ROs). In addition, many others had to be formally trained as *appraisers*, and a bureaucracy had to be set up to administer the processes involved. This inevitably bureaucratic response to the need to ensure quality has been very time-consuming. However, these processes do help in many ways by emphasising accountability and the need to keep up to date. Good doctors working in good organisations have always kept up to date with their skills and with the evidence base in their areas of practice. Good doctors in poor organisations have often found it hard to find the time (and funding) for these activities. Now that it is mandated from the top down, healthcare organisations find it hard (but not impossible) to refuse time and money for appropriate continuing professional development.

To return to the point that by themselves bureaucratic measures do not work, let us consider an example from another field. There are recurrent scandals about childcare, usually focusing on the failure of social workers and healthcare workers to detect abuse and act appropriately. Again, the response tends to be bureaucratic with enquiries that produce long lists of recommendations. Inspectorates 'ensure' the recommendations are followed, at least on paper. The culture tends to be one of fear, restricted autonomy, alienation and form-filling. Often departments are under-resourced for the work they are expected to do, and even if they have resources the 'atmosphere' makes it hard to attract good staff. To some extent, these considerations also apply in the NHS.

Good leadership and management is about changing this atmosphere; about changing the culture from high-blame, top-down command and control to one where professionals exercise their skills with an appropriate degree of autonomy whilst working with a shared purpose and understanding. This attracts people to work in the organisation and to take responsibility. It is this kind of culture change that makes the real difference and that requires good leadership if it is to be developed and sustained. Doctors in management have an opportunity for creating a positive culture amongst medical staff through their roles in the appraisal and job planning cycle and their role in managing performance.

If these areas are not handled well, they can also lead to demoralisation and difficulties in retaining staff.

APPRAISAL AND JOB PLANNING

Appraisal and job planning go hand in hand. Developmental needs identified through appraisal, for example, will relate to what is in the job plan. The job plan will also need to be realistic for the doctor to do a good job.

Appraisal

The Department of Health website originally stated that the primary aim of NHS appraisal was to identify personal and professional development needs. Preparation for the annual appraisal meeting and the appraisal itself certainly should have a developmental aspect. Appraisal can, however, also be seen as a tool for performance management. In other words, it can be a summative process. In some settings, there is an element of reward (bonus) for achieving targets. In medical appraisal, the summative element concerns whether a doctor is maintaining their knowledge and skills (including interpersonal skills) at an appropriate level. These targets for continuing professional development are agreed at the appraisal meeting. Medical appraisers undergo special training to ensure that the process is properly and fairly carried through and are usually doctors that are not part of the formal medical management structure, ensuring a degree of independence.

In the UK, the GMC provides a framework for appraisal and revalidation. Doctors are revalidated on a 5-year cycle based on the recommendation of the relevant RO. Medical Directors are usually designated as ROs under the GMC framework. ROs need to satisfy themselves that appraisals on an annual basis over the 5-year cycle, together with information from the organisation's clinical governance system, meet the required standards to recommend individual doctors for revalidation. As part of this process, doctors have to obtain formal feedback from colleagues (clinicians, managers and other staff) and patients, thus giving a rounded view of their performance (360-degree appraisal) as well as information about training, contributions to Quality Improvement such as audit work and information about serious and other incidents.

The format of annual appraisals for doctors is clearly specified, but individual trusts have their own commercially sourced online systems and appraisal in primary care is co-ordinated by NHS England. In Wales and Scotland, there are national online systems (with the enticing acronyms MARS [Medical Appraisal Revalidation System] and SOAR [Scottish Online Appraisal Resource]: see Further Reading). We do not want to go into details here about National schemes or GMC requirements. We want instead to discuss how medical managers can

- Make appraisal as beneficial as possible
- Encourage a culture of personal development
- Encourage personal responsibility and accountability

- Ensure the whole process (including job planning) is used to facilitate alignment between the goals of the organisation and the goals of the individual

The alternative is 'going through the motions' in a lifeless (and unpleasant) process of (online) form-filling followed by a seemingly pointless interview with an appraiser.

Doctors are generally highly motivated to help other people. If we set up the appraisal and job-planning process so that it strengthens this motivation, we will do better than if we set up a more authoritarian performance management culture where the doctor is seen as a reluctant performer. To achieve maximum benefit, the appraisal–continuing professional development cycle needs to be set in a culture where the appraiser focuses on supporting the doctor's professional development, encouraging personal responsibility and accountability. The appraisal meeting is not the place to raise issues of poor performance. These should be dealt with outside of the annual appraisal meeting, and if they come to light during an appraisal meeting, the meeting may have to adjourn to enable them to be properly addressed.

An annual appraisal gives people a great opportunity to reflect on the year looking at

- Clinical and other work
- Continuing professional development
- Relationships with patients
- Relationships with colleagues
- Relationships with managers
- Mismatch between organisational expectations and resources

The appraiser should be willing to listen to the person being appraised, to ask questions designed to elicit self-awareness in the appraisee, to provide accurate feedback (including praise and, where necessary, constructive criticism). Above all, annual appraisal and job planning should be an opportunity for the person being appraised to reflect on their achievements in the last year and plan for the next, including how to deal with any unresolved issues. For some doctors, it could partly be seen as an exercise in supporting and developing EI. A 360-degree appraisal gives the appraisee feedback from a variety of colleagues (doctors, nurses, secretaries, other healthcare professionals, voluntary sector, patients and carers) and is a required part of revalidation. Feedback from the 360-degree appraisal needs to be managed carefully to avoid unwanted negative side effects, and the 360-degree appraisal feeds into the annual appraisal cycle.

Job planning

Though in some organisations this has been done at the same time as appraisal, there are good reasons for keeping them separate. Job planning is essentially the process through which the organisation's and the individual's expectations of each other are agreed. Job plans are usually agreed between the doctor and their medical manager. Appraisal helps clarify personal aspirations and feeds into job planning, and changes in the job plan may create developmental needs which feed into appraisal. Job planning and objectives are essentially an agreement between the employer and the employee and cover such items as timetable, on-call arrangements, professional duties external to the organisation (eg Royal College or Trade Union work), time and resources for continuing professional development and so on. The BMA provides a checklist for hospital doctors to use in job planning [10]. It also provides separate advice for salaried GPs [11].

Job planning and annual appraisal give each doctor a vital opportunity to look at personal, service and organisational objectives for the next year and ensure that they are reasonably aligned.

MANAGING PERFORMANCE

Senior doctors generally manage their own performance. The appraisal and job-planning process gives them, their appraiser and their medical manager an opportunity to review this against agreed goals and standards. If these have not been attained, it is often for systemic reasons. Have there been obstacles that could not be overcome? Have sufficient resources been made available to make the goal realistic? If the goal is still relevant, what can be done to make it more attainable in the coming year? This is a *two-sided* bargain and it is important that both sides work hard to realise agreed goals. Only where doctors are failing to meet objectives despite adequate support from the organisation should the medical manager need to consider what other action might need to be taken.

Underperformance

The risk of underperformance is minimised if the conditions in the workplace are good, with

- Adequate support
- Reasonable workload
- Good relationships
- Shared purpose
- Clarity about responsibilities
- An appropriate degree of autonomy
- An opportunity to exercise skills

As the restructuring within the UK's healthcare system continues, however, the presence of these conditions has inevitably declined, particularly in relation to work intensification and staff shortages in the NHS. Concerns about doctors' performance will come to light through clinical governance procedures, complaints and, occasionally, through annual appraisal, though this last should be the exception rather than the rule.

When an issue concerning the performance of a colleague comes to a medical manager, they need first to determine who the appropriate person is to deal with it. All NHS organisations have carefully thought-out and negotiated policies and procedures that must be followed. The principles that underpin these are generally similar:

- Protect patients from risk.
- Seek advice from human resources managers and (if appropriate) national advisory bodies or (for trainees) the relevant postgraduate training authorities.
- Find out the facts using agreed procedures.
- Decide (in consultation) whether the matter can be dealt with informally.
- If the matter needs to be dealt with formally, decide (in consultation with human resources and appropriate authorities) which procedures (health/ capability/conduct) are appropriate and follow them fairly and swiftly.

In cases where fitness to practice is affected, it is necessary to inform the GMC. Again, national NHS bodies, local procedures and other sources of advice will help in making decisions.

Problems can arise from a variety of sources, broadly classified as health, clinical and behavioural. The National Clinical Advisory Service (NCAS) developed a great deal of expertise in this area and offered useful support. NCAS was subsumed into the NHS litigation authority, which in turn has been absorbed into *NHS Resolution* whose website (https://www.resolution.nhs.uk) will become fully active in 2018. There are separate arrangements for dealing with NHS litigation in Scotland.

RELATIONSHIPS WITH MANAGERS

Managers in health and social care are a diverse group. They are often drawn from the ranks of the clinical professions into general management roles. The advantages this brings are considerable. Hopefully, they understand some of the complexities of real-life clinical care and hopefully they still have some of the patient-centred ethos that characterises the clinical professions at their best. Increasingly however, general managers, human resources managers and other specialists are drawn from the graduate population through the NHS management training schemes. Their basic degree will be in business studies or a related discipline and they will often be studying for a diploma or Master's degree in health service management and leadership. Clearly people coming through this route will have more initial training in management and may well have competences and skills that the manager coming through the clinical route traditionally acquired over time through practice. They may, in their training, be exposed to clinical situations as they help manage projects on waiting lists, turnover and so on, but they will have to work harder than managers who have come from clinical backgrounds to gain genuine empathy for the reality of complex and often unpredictable clinical work.

The distinctions between administration, management and leadership are useful here (see Chapter 1). Remember, good administration means doing routine tasks well, good management involves making things happen even when the environment is complex and good leadership means helping a group or organisation find its direction *and* drawing the best out of people to serve a common purpose. At a less senior level, managers may be concerned with a mixture of administrative, leadership, management and clinical tasks (eg the ward manager). At an intermediate level (except in medicine), the clinical work disappears and administration and management predominate. This is the level at which non-clinical graduate managers enter. At more senior levels still, administrative and managerial skills remain important foundations, but leadership ability becomes increasingly important. Senior managers will have specialist knowledge, skills and competences, for example, in finance or human resources. Medical Directors, Directors of Nursing and Clinical Directors retain strong links to their professions of origin.

With such a diverse group there can be few generalisations. Working relationships must be based on general principles. What makes effective relationships at work? You will remember the list from the previous chapter:

- Mutual respect
- Shared vision (and mission)
- Shared values
- Clear definitions of roles and responsibilities
- Flexibility (within limits)
- Integrity

Senior managers need these principles as much as anybody else. Indeed, they need to model them for the whole organisation.

At Board level, it is important for people to know enough of each other's functions to exercise corporate responsibility. This does not mean that the Medical Director needs to know as much about accounting as the Finance Director or as much about personnel management as the Human Resources Rirector. However, he or she needs to know enough to contribute responsibly to decision-making and enough to know when to ask for help from fellow directors in operational decisions.

RELATIONSHIPS WITH PEOPLE WHO USE OUR SERVICES (AND THEIR CAREGIVERS/FAMILIES)

Medical managers will have been accustomed to relating to patients as service users. Now they will have to relate to them in other roles, too. They will have to relate to them as representatives on various decision-making bodies, as colleagues in managing various projects and, occasionally as complainants or even as litigants. The last two roles demand a degree of reserve and caution that may not come naturally to the clinician in these informal days.

Service user representatives, patients and family caregivers will often form natural alliances with clinical managers. They sometimes carry more influence with decision-makers than clinicians so that making sure they are well informed and seeking their views and their support becomes an important part of securing improvements in the service.

As complainants, service users deserve to be treated with respect and frankness. If an informal complaint is dealt with respectfully *and* effectively, it will often not develop into a formal complaint. The legal system in the UK is (with the exception of coroners' courts) 'adversarial'. Unfortunately, complaints can develop into litigation and those dealing with complaints often feel limited by considerations of what will happen if litigation follows. This is another reason for dealing with complaints at an early, informal stage whenever possible. Clinicians need to be aware if patients or relatives are dissatisfied with the service they are receiving and to take reasonable steps to deal with any concerns. Martin Luther King once said 'violence is the voice of the unheard'. In a similar way, the formal complaint is often the result of people feeling that their concerns have not been properly 'heard' and dealt with.

Senior medical managers should do all they can to ensure that clinical staff are sensitive to patients' and relatives' concerns and are empowered and competent to deal with them before they develop into complaints. This is an important aspect of leadership. When a formal complaint does arise, it is dealt with by a formal process which rarely leaves all parties feeling that they have been fairly treated. Medical managers will have various roles in this process. The Medical Director will see the results of investigations following complaints that involve doctors and may help in the drafting of the formal response that is sent to the complainant. Some medical staff will be trained as case investigators and will report to the Medical Director acting as case manager for complaints involving a doctor. Another important role for the medical manager is to make sure that doctors who are complained against receive appropriate support throughout the process of handling the complaint. Additionally, the manager may need to arrange further training or support arising from the outcome of the complaint. Rarely, disciplinary action against doctors may follow, and the Medical Director will have to make a decision about this. For this reason, senior medical managers need to remain unprejudiced during any formal investigation of conduct. Doctors involved in complaints should also be aware of and comply with any 'lessons learned', action plans and service redesigns resulting from the complaint or Serious Incident. Duty of Candour is also important, and medical and other staff should work in a transparent way and keep service users and/or carers informed about actions or omissions that led to some form of harm.

People who need health services ('patients' or potential patients) are the reason for the existence of health services, clinicians and medical managers. Being 'patient-centred' is the common ground on which managers and clinicians can and should come together. Unfortunately, the strong central direction of modern health services has caused some people working in the service to be more concerned with reaching 'targets' than with the real needs of patients. Of course, if the targets were perfectly patient-centred this would not cause any conflict. Unfortunately, central targets can sometimes be difficult to adapt to local circumstances and that is one of the many challenges facing medical managers.

The pressure to further commercialise the NHS in recent years has been accompanied by a relative reduction in investment and has generated its own distractions from patient-centred care. The important thing, in the face of all political and managerial fashions and imperatives, is to keep the needs of service users central and to develop the alliance between patients and the clinical professions that ultimately serve *them*, not the organisation.

RELATIONSHIPS, RELATIONSHIPS, RELATIONSHIPS

In the end, given adequate clinical and managerial competency in the more technical areas, the ability to develop and sustain high-quality relationships between doctors, managers, other professionals and workers and patients remains a vital and pivotal foundation for good practice and good management.

REFERENCES

1. Goleman S (2004) *Emotional Intelligence and Working with Emotional Intelligence.* London, UK: Bloomsbury Publishing.
2. Berne E (2016) *Games People Play: The Psychology of Human Relationships.* London, UK: Penguin Life.
3. Morgan G (2006) *Images of Organisations.* London, UK: SAGE Publications.
4. Solomon C (2003) Transactional analysis theory: The basics. *Transactional Analysis Journal,* 33: 15–22.
5. Rath B and Conchie T (2009) *Strengths Based Leadership.* Washington, DC: Gallup Press.
6. Covey SR (2016) *The 7 Habits of Highly Effective People.* London, UK: FranklinCovey, Mango Media Inc. (Kindle Edition).
7. Kenney C (2015) *A Leadership Journey in Health Care: Virginia Mason's Story.* Boca Raton, FL: CRC Press.
8. Department of Health (1998) *Clinical Governance: Moving from Rhetoric to Reality.* London, UK: Department of Health.
9. Alderwick H, Dunn P, McKenna H, Walsh N and Ham C (2016) *Sustainability and Transformation Plans in the NHS: How Are They Being Developed in Practice?* London, UK: The King's Fund.
10. British Medical Association (2016) Job planning checklist for consultants, medical academics and SAS doctors. https://www.bma.org.uk/advice/employment /job-planning/job-plan-checklist (accessed 15 October 2017).
11. British Medical Association (2016) Job planning: Guidance for practitioners. https://www.bma.org.uk/advice/employment/job-planning/job -planning-guidance-for-gps (accessed 28 March 2018).

FURTHER READING AND USEFUL RESOURCES

GMC framework for medical appraisal and revalidation. http://www.gmc-uk.org/doctors/revalidation/revalidation_gmp_framework.asp (accessed 28 November 2017).

Medical appraisal England. https://www.england.nhs.uk/medical-revalidation/appraisers/med-app-guide/ (accessed 16 October 2017).

Medical appraisal Scotland. http://www.appraisal.nes.scot.nhs.uk/ (accessed 16 October 2017).

Medical appraisal Wales. https://medical.marswales.org/ (accessed 28 April 2018).

Transactional analysis (TA). http://www.ericberne.com/transactional-analysis/ (accessed 28 November 2017).

3

Understanding your organisation

Health services are often complex organisations that are difficult to understand, partly because of the ever-changing context within which they operate. The British National Health Service (NHS) is the organisation that the authors are most familiar with and it is no exception. In fact, since political devolution of control of health services to Wales and Scotland, different parts of the UK health service have developed in different ways, so that one can no longer refer to the NHS as a whole.

There are many different tools for understanding organisations and a brief, practical text like this cannot aim to be comprehensive. Instead, we will follow a pragmatic approach with a brief historical account of the NHS followed by two different perspectives taken from the work of Morgan [4] and Handy [5]. Although the context is British, the influences on healthcare systems are now global and so the same principles can be applied to understanding any health system:

- Historical development
- Use of metaphors to enhance understanding
- Especially understanding the different cultures within the organisation and within which the organisation functions

UNDERSTANDING YOUR ORGANISATION IN CONTEXT

The British NHS came into being in 1948, after the Second World War. It was essentially shaped on mechanistic or bureaucratic lines with a top-down 'command and control' structure. Control was partly by central government through Regional Boards, partly by local executive committees (general practitioners, opticians, dentists and pharmacies) and partly by local government (public health and ambulance services). Teaching hospitals retained a degree of independence with their own Boards of Governors. The centralised structure was modelled on the Emergency Medical Service which had performed well in the face of the disruption and casualties caused by the bombing of cities during the Second World War. There were incremental changes over many years.

Then, in the 1990s, under the influence of economic theorists from Europe and the USA, there was a fundamental change with the introduction of a market-oriented system with a purchaser–provider split, at least at the secondary care level. A service ethos was partly replaced by a market ethos, where organisations competed for customers (patients) via their GPs and where financial efficiency was the bottom line. After a brief respite, the process of introducing market forces continued in England in the form of 'World Class Commissioning' and Primary Care Trusts (PCTs) that purchased health services from provider organisations. By this time the devolved administrations in Scotland, Wales and Northern Ireland were responsible for the NHS in their separate nations and were generally pursuing less radical market-oriented policies. Meanwhile, in England the 2012 Health and Social Care Act was followed by the creation of 211 Clinical Commissioning Groups (CCGs) in community health services and secondary care.

In response to the NHS deficit, in 2014 the Chief Executive of the NHS in England, Simon Stevens proposed *A Five Year Forward View*, which aims to maintain quality services through innovation and cost savings in return for additional governmental funding by 2020/2021. A key part of this plan is the creation of Sustainability and Transformation Plans (STPs), 44 'local health systems' clustered in acute and specialist care, which represent the main bulk of the NHS deficit, tasked with creating 'footprints' for planning and delivering care. If they manage to do this in 2016/2017, they can access £2.1bn of 'transformation' funding, not actually new money but part of the £10bn NHS funding agreed in the 2015 spending review. The main bulk of this £2.1bn will go to emergency care, and smaller pots for efficiencies and transformations in service delivery.

Concerns have been raised by local NHS support groups about the timescale and transparency of how STPs are managed. One of the problems is that STPs are massive structures covering on average 1.2 million people, merging local authorities and CCGs. The timescale for the creation of STPs has been criticised as the final STP Delivery Plans were supposed to be submitted on the 21st October 2016, just weeks after their creation. These full plans were not published, rather they were sent to NHS England for revisions and on the 23rd December 2016, CCGs had to sign 2-year operational contracts with providers, starting on the 1st April 2017. Even for the most committed local health campaigner if you knew about these deadlines, the chances of organising a genuine consultation around them were extremely unlikely.

Accountable Care Organisations (ACOs) are proposed. They will take a variety of forms. In return for a contract that lasts for some years, they will take responsibility for the provision of all health services in the geographical area. Though integration of services makes sense, ACOs may be forced to cut services and private providers may put profit before patients. At the time of this printing, the legality of these ACOs is being challenged in the courts. This 'cuts-dressed-as-innovation' is familiar to those clinicians who were involved in the creation of CCGs where cuts in budgets were combined with devolution of healthcare provision to the local level. The task of balancing the NHS's books in one year while at the same time improving patient care is potentially an impossible task, leaving STPs with the risk of debt or gaming of performance data. The STPs however have produced some innovative ideas, some of which are discussed in Chapter 8.

GOVERNANCE AND MANAGEMENT ISSUES IN THE ENGLISH NHS

Procedurally, commissioners were helped in their tasks by various organisations like the National Mental Health Development Unit and the National Institute for Health and Clinical Excellence (NICE), which set standards and approved treatments for NHS use at the (English) national level, with different arrangements in different parts of the UK. The tension between the old 'service model' and the new 'commissioner-provider' model was high in the area of service design. The old system tended to rely on the expertise of local clinicians, especially consultants. The new system relied on evidence abstracted at a higher level through organisations like NICE. There was a potential for more superficial uniformity but perhaps at the expense of innovation and inspired local clinical leadership. Whether or not the ACOs currently proposed will reconcile the two models remains to be seen.

In an attempt to ensure that standards were maintained, there were inspectorates (the Care Quality Commission, in its latest incarnation) and (for 'Foundation Trusts' and mainly for financial governance matters) 'Monitor'. Monitor and a number of other bodies and functions (the NHS Trust Development Authority, the National Reporting and Learning System, the Advancing Change team and the Intensive Support Teams) were absorbed in 2016 into a new organisation, 'NHS Improvement'.

The inadequacy of the initial arrangements was brought into sharp focus in 2009 when the Mid-Staffordshire NHS Trust, in its anxiety to achieve Foundation status, concentrated on financial savings and not on a marked excess mortality, possibly at least in part due to some of the cuts. An investigation by the Healthcare Commission (the predecessor to the Care Quality Commission) found, among other failings, that the Trust had shed too many clinical staff in an effort to balance the books. From the narrow point of view of Monitor, they succeeded, being granted Foundation Status just before the Healthcare Commission commenced its inquiry. Nor did the Healthcare Commission come out of the episode covered in glory. The excess mortality was first picked up by an independent public health monitoring body called 'Dr Foster' (www.drfosterintelligence.co.uk/), not by the Commission. There have been five reports into the Mid-Staffordshire scandal (summarised by Campbell [1]) including one under the NHS Act [2] and a full public inquiry [3]. Whether the new governance arrangements for NHS England set up under NHS Improvement will really improve things remains to be seen.

Most people who work in healthcare in England consider themselves to be employed by the NHS. However, through the growth of private providers, a growing number of healthcare professionals are working for private contractors, third sector organisations, private employment agencies or enjoy a dubious status of 'self-employed'. For example, according to the National Council of Voluntary Organisations (NCVO), an estimated 437,000 third sector workers are employed in health and social care with 115,000 in residential care. This raises important management issues for doctors, where a growing number of team members will not be directly employed by the NHS and will be operating within their own separate management systems.

All of these changes have raised public concerns about the governance and management of this complex system of commissioning and private providers within the NHS with longstanding campaigns aimed to 'save' the NHS. Additionally, these changes and managing transitions to ever-changing systems and structures will demand a great deal of skill and flexibility from doctors and managers in both primary and secondary care organisations. When we examine the flux and transformation metaphors of organisation later in this chapter, the relevance of the political and economic context may be evident.

METAPHORS AS A FRAMEWORK FOR UNDERSTANDING

The task for the medical manager is first of all to understand his or her own service, how this fits into the organisation to which it belongs; then to understand how the organisation fits into the wider healthcare system. We use many concepts in trying to understand organisations, but one of the most powerful is metaphor. Gareth Morgan [4] discusses eight powerful metaphors that help us to understand organisations (see Box 3.1).

All these metaphors can help us to understand an organisation (and they all have limitations). Good doctor-managers will seek to take a number of different

---

BOX 3.1: Morgan's metaphors of organisations

- Organisations as machines
- Organisations as organisms
- Organisations as brains: Learning and self-organisation
- Organisations as cultures: Creating social reality
- Organisations as political systems: Interests, conflicts and power
- Organisations as psychic prisons
- Organisation as flux and transformation
- Organisations as instruments of domination

points of view as they grapple with an organisational problem. Other metaphors will occur, too, such as organisational diagnosis and treatment. There is no space here to explore all the metaphors, and too many different perspectives can be confusing. We have selected two of the most pertinent to modern health services to discuss in more detail:

1. Organisations as cultures
2. Organisation as flux and transformation

This is not arbitrary. One of the authors found the first of these particularly useful when he first moved into medical management because it helped him see that different parts of the NHS have different cultures, implying different modes of operation, motivators, success criteria and timescales. The second is chosen because it is the one most doctors instantly recognise as relevant to ever-changing modern health services.

ORGANISATIONAL CULTURE

The idea of management cultures first came to prominence following the phenomenal success of Japanese industry after the Second World War. Academics who studied management realised that there were cultural factors at work. Another, more topical, example is the 'bonus culture' in banks that preceded the financial crash of 2008. In this case it is possible to make a case that traces the diffusion of American child-rearing practice first into American commercial culture and then into the global marketplace. The idea is very simple. Wanted behaviour should be rewarded, preferably with tangible rewards. So, the theorist might argue, the practice of giving children sweets for being good led to the practice of giving fund managers bonuses for doing their job 'well' (ie securing short-term profits). Fuelled by greed, this led to ever–more complex schemes for 'making money' and then to disaster. Culture can be very powerful.

Charles Handy is sometimes described as the only 'home-grown' British 'management guru'. (In fact, he was born in Ireland.) Indeed, the term 'management guru' was allegedly coined by a journalist to describe him. Writing at the end of the twentieth century in a book that has been re-issued several times [5], he described four dominant cultures in modern organisations. He identified each with a god from Greek mythology (reflecting his own classical education). His scheme is undoubtedly over-simplistic but is still incredibly helpful in understanding why different bits of the organisation behave in different ways and the ways in which overall political culture influences healthcare developments. Handy also proposed a theory of 'cultural propriety' that suggests that all the cultures are equally valid but that each has its place.

Table 3.1 lists some of the attributes of the four cultures described by Handy.

Handy's book includes a questionnaire for individuals to look at their own cultural preferences and those of their organisations.

Table 3.1 Charles Handy's dominant cultures of organisations

'God' and culture	Attributes	Best suited to	Control and influence
Zeus: the 'club' culture	Based on knowing (the top) people, makes speedy, intuitive decisions	Small entrepreneurial (often family) businesses. Also found at senior levels in politics!	Personal praise or punishment from the 'boss'. Who you know is more important than what you know
Apollo: the 'role' culture	Related to the 'machine' metaphor essentially sees people, according to their roles, as replaceable parts in the organisation	Routine tasks where change is minimal and unexpected variation unusual; surprisingly common in the NHS given the amount and pace of change	Impersonal exercise of economic and political power to enforce standards and procedures. Room size, desk size, car size = 'status'
Athena: the 'task' culture	Focus on the continual and successful definition and solution of problems	Team working to solve problems where complexity and variety are common. A common culture for the clinician. May waste time/ resources in routine settings	Personal commitment to the task, rewarded by success. Team members valued for their competences rather than who they know or their role 'labels'
Dionysus: the 'existential' or 'craft' culture	Focus on enabling Dionysians to achieve their purpose	Situations where individual talents or skills are most important. Also found in clinical practice	Enjoyment intrinsic to the exercise of skills (which may include meeting the needs of others)

Source: Handy, C., The Gods of Management, Souvenir Press, London, UK, 2009.

EXERCISE 3.1
Organisational cultures

Consider your own organisation. How does it work at various levels? If you work in a clinical team, does the team subdivide to tackle the tasks around the individual needs of patients or are you more a collection of individualists, each exercising their own skills in the service of patients but without much coordination? Do different disciplines in the team work according to different models? What about the immediate organisation you work for? How important is the enforcement of standards and procedures? Do conflicts arise between different cultures? How much scope is there for team working? Are people expected to enjoy their work? How does your organisation compare with the wider health service in terms of its dominant 'gods'? How do your own cultural expectations mesh with those of the organisation?

Consider how appropriate different cultures are for different tasks. How do Athenians or Dionysians feel in an Apollonian organisation? What are the vices and virtues of each culture? If you really want to get a grip on this, have a look at the book *The Gods of Management* [5] and try the questionnaire in the chapter on 'the gods at work'. Doctors working in the health service often see themselves as Athenians or Dionysians working in organisations that are still predominantly Apollonian. This causes tension. Figure 3.1 illustrates the recent management structure of the NHS from two different perspectives; the first (Figure 3.1a) is a 'top-down' organisation chart; the second (Figure 3.1b) is a patient-centered team culture that usually works at the clinical level. Both these illustrations have validity. The first is keener in terms of issues of responsibility and accountability. The second perspective accords with 'messy reality'.

Figure 3.1b illustrates how clinicians of all disciplines work within their provider organisations and in collaboration with a wider network of other providers to help people resolve their health problems. The complexity (and cost) of interventions may vary from the prescription of an antibiotic to treat an uncomplicated bacterial infection in primary care to the co-ordinated provision of care and treatment for people with enduring and disabling physical and mental illness. The focus is on bringing together the right resources to efficiently meet patients' needs. This way of conceptualising the organisation resembles the 'onion' model developed in Oxfordshire and discussed briefly in Chapter 8. The actual future structure of the NHS in England is in flux with the STP proposals for 'footprints' and ACOs and the details of these illustrations, especially the top-down role culture chart, will change. Clinicians may not see much of the healthcare system beyond the parts that are needed for 'their' patients. Although sometimes acting as individuals, they are part of an essentially 'team' culture.

However, doctors in management need to have a wider appreciation of the culture(s) of the health service. Handy does not suggest that one culture is 'better'

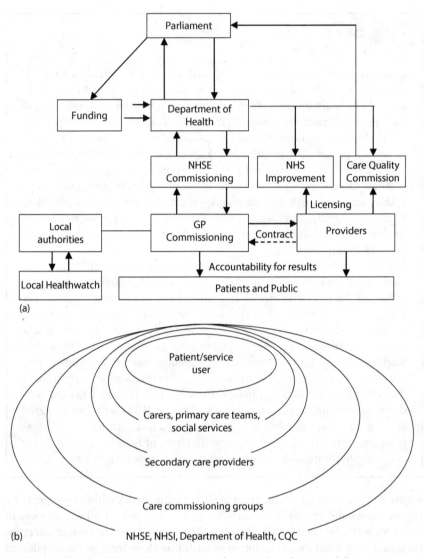

Figure 3.1 The English NHS (a) as a (top-down) role culture and (b) as a (patient-centred) team culture.

than another. He speaks of 'cultural appropriateness'. Thus, a role culture may be good at regular, repetitive tasks such as paying all our salaries but hopeless at dealing with the complexities of a real-life clinical emergency where the team culture is generally most appropriate. Problems arise when the different cultures do not know their place in the wider scheme of things. One of the tasks for a medical manager is to ensure that cultural appropriateness is not violated. Another task is to understand the different cultures and their different languages ('jargon') so as to be able to adequately represent one to the other without misunderstanding.

Another way at looking at cultures in healthcare is to examine the development of health services in the UK in the last century. Before the NHS there was a market culture, supplemented by various forms of insurance and the individual charitable donation of time to 'the poor' by some doctors and organisations. The early NHS was predominantly a top-down organisation with strong elements of role culture but with clinicians relatively free to function independently. We have called this a 'service culture'. Then, under the influence of economic and political theorists, the internal market was introduced, here described as the 'commissioner-provider' culture. This was designed to remedy the so-called 'producer capture' where the 'workers' of public service industries were (somewhat insultingly) seen as running the business for their own benefit. Gains in efficiency were also predicted (though the long-term efficiency of markets must now be in some doubt). Finally, running alongside this evolution, we have the wider phenomenon of the consumer culture. Table 3.2 gives a simplified account of the characteristics of these different cultures. As the English NHS evolves, the consumer model, as presented here, is essentially a market model with service commissioners acting as moderators and purchasers of service on behalf of consumers.

Ezekiel Emanuel and Linda Emanuel [6], in a classical paper, described four models of the 'physician–patient' relationship. The *paternalistic* model is the traditional model in which doctor uses their skills to determine the diagnosis and best

Table 3.2 Evolution and development of dominant cultures in health services

Culture	Market	Service	Commissioner-provider	Consumer
Who 'knows' best?	Buyer	Provider	Commissioner	Service user
Who disposes of resources?	Buyer	Provider	Commissioner	Service user limited by commissioner
Who is in charge?	Buyer	Provider	Commissioner	Service user (in theory!)
Some potential advantages:	Good for those with lots of money	Providers *do know* more. Demands altruism in workers to work well	Interests of different stakeholders considered	Service user is 'empowered'
Some potential disadvantages:	Bad for those who are poor	'Producer capture' – run in interest of workers, not users	Costly extra layers of management. Duplication of supporting functions	Costly extra layers of management. Service user empowerment may be illusory

management and presents the patient with selective information that encourages them to consent to the doctor's diagnosis and 'treatment'. In the *informative* model (also known as the *consumer* model), the doctor provides the consumer/patient with all relevant information and leaves the decision about what to do next to the patient. In the *interpretive* model, the doctor assists the patient to understand their own values and seeks to order diagnostic tests and treatment in line with these values. In the *deliberative* (or co-operative/co-productive) model, the doctor seeks to help the patient to find the best health-related values for the clinical situation, engaging the patient in dialogue on what course of action is best. In the pre-NHS and early NHS years, the *paternalistic* model was probably dominant. Currently the *consumer* model is more dominant and in some areas co-production of health is recognised as increasingly important.

ORGANISATION AS FLUX AND TRANSFORMATION

Since the 1990s the NHS has been in a state of continuous flux and change. The ideas ('logics of change') that Morgan uses to give insight into this metaphor are as follows:

- *Autopoesis*: A new way at looking at organisational relationships with their environment
- *Chaos and complexity theory*: How ordered patterns can emerge from spon-taneous self-organisation
- *Cybernetics*: Exploring the way change is 'enfolded' in circular relations
- *The dialectic dimension*: Change as a function of tensions between opposites

Autopoeisis

The conventional logic of systems theory sees the organisation as a system within an environment to which it needs to respond. It is helpful and is seen in various techniques, including the following:

- 'STEP' analysis, where an organisation systematically looks at the social, technical, economic and political factors in the environment that need to be considered in planning its business.
- 'SWOT' analysis, where the strengths, weaknesses, opportunities and threats to an organisation seen as an organism reacting to an outside environment are explored (see Chapter 6 for more details).

Autopoiesis (another biologically derived metaphor) suggests that organisations are essentially self-referential. An organisation's interaction with the 'environ-ment' is really a reflection and part of its own organisation. It interacts with the environment in a way that favours its own survival and 'self-production'. All parts of the wider system (around which it is impossible to draw realistic boundaries) influence other parts in a reflexive and mutually dependent way. Morgan gives the biological example of the honeybee. Bees are linked with botanical, agricultural, animal, human and social systems. Eliminate the bee and we all go hungry! Each element of a well-functioning system combines the maintenance of itself with the maintenance of other parts of the system. Thus, the commissioners and different providers have their niches and are not necessarily in a race for 'survival of the fittest' as suggested by more simplistic analyses. 'Egocentric' organisations tend to ignore or undervalue this systemic wisdom. The autopoietic metaphor also helps explain why organisations providing health services tend to evolve with the body politic. It explains the shift from service to market philosophies as socialism has become nearly as unpopular in the UK as in the USA. The collapse of the financial markets in 2008 from greed and over-complexity may also bring more general societal changes, which will be reflected in healthcare systems (see next section).

Chaos, complexity and cybernetics

Chaos theory and complexity theory provide further insight into how organisations behave in real life. Complex organisations are characterised by multiple systems of interaction that are at once ordered and chaotic. Random events can produce massive reverberations in the system with consequent chaos. Nevertheless, order reasserts itself. A good example would be the global economic crisis of 2008/2009. Here the effects of sub-prime mortgages in the USA destabilised a system that had been made over-complicated by traders seeking to maximise their own bonuses. Eventually order will reassert itself. Whether it will be the 'old order' of under-regulated global market capitalism, or whether a more regulated order will supervene, or whether some completely new approach will prove most attractive remains (at the time of writing) to be seen.

Medical managers often have to deal with unexpected events that appear 'random' in their timing if not in their actual occurrence. These include doctors falling ill or misbehaving, complaints, politically motivated changes in the organisation of the service, epidemics and many other events. Just as the behaviour of a flock of birds or a shoal of fish can be modelled on a computer by a set of simple rules, so we can bring ourselves through the apparent chaos and complexity of the healthcare system by holding on to a few simple principles of 'good management practice'.

EXERCISE 3.2
Learning lessons

Consider some of the difficult management situations you have faced. Write a brief account of what happened. What were the learning points? What principles did you use to guide you through the situation? What new principles (if any) did you learn? How do these principles relate to your core values as a doctor? The General Medical Council (GMC) guidance for doctors in management [7] may help. Do you have the same or different core values as a non-medical manager? (See the *Code of Conduct for NHS Managers*, [8].)

Dialectics

This is essentially a philosophical (and political) theory that change emerges out of a *synthesis* between a *thesis* and an *antithesis*. In politics, the tension between opposing theories and viewpoints produces an emergent new order. The relationship between this and chaos/complexity theory is obvious.

PRACTICAL APPLICATIONS

In the midst of complexity, we need to do the following [1]:

- Rethink what we mean by organisations and how they are 'controlled'.
- Learn the art of managing and changing contexts.
- Learn how to use small changes to achieve large effects.
- Live with continual transformation and emergent order.
- Be open to new ideas.

Changing contexts

A good example of an attempt to manage by changing contexts was the introduction of clinical governance into the NHS. Corporate governance and financial probity were early targets in the formation of NHS Trusts. Then the concept of *clinical governance* was introduced 'to create an environment in which clinical excellence will flourish'. The idea was to change the context so that clinical excellence was as important to the boards of NHS Trusts as was financial probity. (The example of the mid-Staffordshire Foundation Trust, cited earlier, suggests the message may not have been well received in all areas.) A good part of health service management can be seen as creating a reasonably stable environment for clinicians of all disciplines to do their jobs. Within this metaphor, *the fundamental role of managers is to create contexts in which appropriate forms of self-organisation can occur.* Morgan actually cites the organisation of a hospital emergency department as an example where managers need to provide a stable and resilient context within which clinicians of all disciplines can self-organise to meet a variety of very different and sometimes complex challenges.

Small changes to achieve large effects

When a system resists change, for example, the move from hospital-dominated 'clinics' to community assessment and treatment in psychiatry, one effective small change can be to harness the enthusiasm of a small group to run a successful 'pilot'. By demonstrating that different ways of working are possible, this can pave the way for larger-scale changes. However, one should never underestimate the power of old patterns of working to reassert themselves. In the specialty of old-age psychiatry, familiar to two of the authors, the pattern of home assessment by senior medical staff was an important shift from the outpatient model of assessment. However, as teams and 'new ways of working' have developed, much of the community assessment is carried out by non-medical members of the team, with doctors (perhaps appropriately) partly retreating to conduct their assessments in clinic settings (which has advantages and disadvantages).

EXERCISE 3.3
Planning for change

Look at the area you are responsible for. Find an area where you would like to make a modest change and consider how the previous principles could be applied. If appropriate, make and carry-through a plan. If the change looks too daunting, look at the section on leading and managing change in Chapter 8 for further ideas.

Living with change and emergent order

Whether or not the churning of repeated reorganisation is a benefit to the health service, it is certainly something that health service managers and clinicians have had to learn to live with over many years. To some extent it can be seen as a consequence of the political imperative to take initiatives designed to win public support (and, perhaps, elections). Some of us may look back with nostalgia on the relatively slow pace of change whilst the post-war political consensus on the service culture of the NHS held. However, nostalgia is not helpful to those who have to manage within the present context. Perhaps the crisis in financial markets alluded to above will eventually lead to a rethink about the current direction in the English NHS, but it hasn't happened yet. Either way, change seems likely to continue, largely driven by politics and the media as well as by emerging technology. In these circumstances managers have to learn to live with change and to influence it for the benefit of patients.

A key issue here is to resist the feeling of disempowerment that comes with too much centrally directed change. Some years ago, it was popular to speak of the 'judo' theory of management where one used the momentum of imposed change to 'throw' things in the direction one wanted them to follow. This is a helpful metaphor for the modern NHS. The medical manager needs to have clear principles and direction The GMC guidance, *Leadership and Management for All Doctors* [7], makes a good starting point. Then, whatever change is imposed, the clear principles and direction can be employed to shift the change in the direction one judges to be in the best interests of patients.

CULTURE IS RELATED TO OUTCOME

A recent systematic review [9] has demonstrated an association between organisational and workplace culture and patient outcomes. Braithwaite et al. formulated a hypothesis that positive cultures were related to positive patient outcomes and negative cultures were associated with negative patient outcomes. They described positive cultures as cohesive, supportive, collaborative and inclusive and negative cultures as 'the converse'. After meticulous analysis of a range of papers from diverse areas of medical practice, they concluded that there was a clear association between positive cultures and a wide range of positive patient outcomes. This paper is worth a thorough read and provides good arguments to tackle those who are sceptical about the importance of positive organisational and workplace culture.

REFERENCES

1. Campbell D (2013) Mid staffs scandal: The essential guide. *The Guardian*. https://www.theguardian.com/society/2013/feb/06/mid-staffs-hospital-scandal-guide (accessed 28 November 2017).
2. Francis R (2010) *Independent Inquiry into Care Provided by Mid Staffordshire NHS Foundation Trust*. London, UK: The Stationery Office.
3. Francis R (2013) *Report of the Mid Staffordshire NHS Foundation Trust Public Inquiry*. London, UK: The Stationery Office.
4. Morgan G (2006) *Images of Organizations*. London, UK: SAGE Publications.
5. Handy C (2009) *The Gods of Management*. London, UK: Souvenir Press.
6. Emanuel E and Emanuel L (1992) Four models of the physician-patient relationship. *The Journal of the American Medical Association*, 267(16): 2221–2229.
7. General Medical Council (2002) *Leadership and Management for All Doctors*. London, UK: The GMC. http://www.gmc-uk.org/guidance/ (accessed 30 April 2018).
8. Department of Health (2002) *Code of Conduct for NHS Managers*. London, UK: Department of Health. http://www.nhsemployers.org/~/media/Employers/Documents/Recruit/Code_of_conduct_for_NHS_managers_2002.pdf (accessed 30 April 2018).
9. Braithwaite J, Herkes J, Ludlow K, Testa L and Lamprell G (2017) Association between organisational and workplace cultures, and patient outcomes: Systematic review. *British Medical Journal Open*, 7: e017708.

FURTHER READING

Centre for Health in the Public Interest (2016) *The 2016/2017 Sustainability and Transformation Fund: Why It Is Not Enough and What Are Its Implications for the Provider Sector?* London, UK: CHPI.

Handy C (2005) *Understanding Organisations*. Revised ed. London, UK: Penguin.

Kings Fund (2016) *Clinical Commissioning: GPs in Charge?* London, UK: Kings Fund.

4

Personal vision, values and goals: Alignment with the organisation

WHAT'S IMPORTANT TO YOU? DEVELOPING YOUR 'VISION'

Almost all senior doctors are (or should be) involved in management. The degree of involvement will vary from negotiations with colleagues about 'on-call' commitments or service reorganisation/development, through posts with formal responsibility for aspects of management (eg some aspect of service development) to formal appointments with substantial commitment to management (such as Clinical Directors, Medical Directors Associate Medical Directors, board members of Clinical Commissioning Groups [CCGs]). If you have taken on a formal management role, ask yourself 'Why?' Be honest! Here are some reasons from our own experience:

- A desire to influence the system and make it better for patients
- The fear that somebody else might get the job and not do it as well as you (this may or may not be true)
- A desire to stop bad decisions being made
- Enjoyment of status, power (and enhanced salary)
- A real interest in good leadership and management
- Despair at the perverse effects of repeated health service 'reforms' and the desire to mitigate damage
- Passionate commitment to developing a health market (or returning to a different model!)
- Belief that doctors have a very important role to play in the management of health provision
- Conviction that only with the powerful involvement of clinicians will the system serve the needs of patients/service users
- A choice of management as a 'career pathway'

More-senior management roles may be initially for a fixed term or may be on a rolling contract. In any case it is helpful to develop a personal vision for what you want to achieve and to translate this into goals that can be achieved in a reasonable timescale. Even a newly appointed consultant or principal without 'extra' management responsibilities can benefit from being clear about their vision, values and goals for what they want to achieve on the managerial front in their first year or so in post. Case study 4.1 illustrates this process of developing a vision and goals.

CASE STUDY 4.1: A FOCUSED INTERVENTION IN MEDICAL MANAGEMENT

One of the authors was asked to support medical management (1 day per week) in an organisation that provided mental health services to Grimsby and NE Lincolnshire. At the time the organisation was part of a Primary Care Trust but subsequently became NAViGO (a social enterprise, see Chapter 8). The Medical Director (the only substantive psychiatric consultant in post in the whole organisation!) had died unexpectedly, following an accident, not long after recruiting several new consultants on short-term contracts from the European Union. The vision was to get the medical aspects of the mental health services working effectively again. There was concordance between the values of the author and that of the organisation that focused on providing first-class services for people with mental health problems and enabling them to contribute fully to their own recovery. This vision broke down into a number of very practical goals, some of which are listed in the following:

- Support the induction of the new consultants into the Trust, including an understanding of the organisation of the National Health Service (NHS) and the Trust, Psychiatric Practice and Mental Health Legislation in England and so on.
- Establish and implement policies and procedures for medical employment, leave, continuing professional development, appraisal, job planning and performance management and so on. (There were 'legacy' policies from a previous organisational set-up, but they did not 'fit' the new organisation.)
- Re-establish the Trust as a respected provider of medical education and training.
- Support one locum consultant in gaining access to the specialist register via article 14, a route for non-European qualified specialists and others.
- Develop the consultant workforce to a point where long-term appointments could be made to consultant posts and a substantive Medical Director could be appointed from amongst the consultant body.
- Support the establishment of an enduring culture of co-operation between the medical workforce and the management of the organisation in which the needs of service users were the first priority.

(Continued)

CASE STUDY 4.1: (Continued) A FOCUSED INTERVENTION IN MEDICAL MANAGEMENT

The initial timescale for achieving this was 1–2 years. This was too ambitious! With an incredible amount of support from the Director of Mental Health Services (who subsequently became Chief Executive of NAViGO), the Chief Executive, the medical personnel specialist, administrative and secretarial staff, the consultants themselves and the Medical School and those responsible for medical post-graduate training, these goals (and a number of other important goals that developed over the period) were all achieved within 4 years. In addition, the culture of co-operation meant that special interests of consultants were harnessed to improve the service by developing specialist services for people with borderline personality disorder, eating disorders and family therapy.

Not all management appointments will be so time limited or so circumscribed in their intention. Nevertheless, if you have not already done so, it is worth considering your personal vision for what you can achieve in management over a realistic time period. It may be something as limited (but not necessarily easy) as developing a co-operative culture or establishing a good reputation for training, or it may be a 'higher-order' vision like 'getting the medical aspects of the mental health services working effectively again'. Whatever it is, it will need thinking about and priorities and goals will need to be set. Figure 4.1 illustrates this process graphically. The foundation for any project involving people is relationships and (shared) values. Next comes a realistic appreciation of where we are

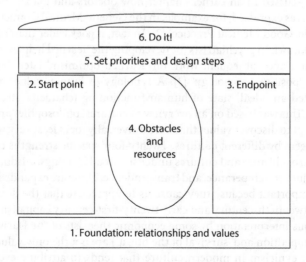

Figure 4.1 Planning to achieve your vision or goals.

and where we want to be (the 'vision'). After this it is necessary to consider the possible obstacles and the resources needed to achieve the vision (after which the endpoint may need to be revised to a more realistic position!). Finally, the tasks needed to achieve the goal/vision need to be prioritised and steps need to be designed, ideally with timings sketched in.

EXERCISE 4.1
Realising your vision

What is your vision for what you want to achieve in the management field in your current post? (This corresponds to the first of Stephen Covey's 7 Habits [1]: being proactive.) This prevents the disappointment inherent in always reacting to other people's initiatives. State this vision as succinctly as possible and decide on a realistic date for achieving it. (This corresponds to the second habit: 'begin with the end in mind'.) Look at the gap between where you are now and where you want to be. Consider what resources are needed to achieve the change (this may be good quality relationships, alliances and communications as much as, or more than, financial resources.) Think about likely obstacles and how they can be negotiated. Prioritise and break the vision down into goals that are manageable and time limited. (This corresponds to the third habit: 'first things first'.)

Start progressing towards your goals, keeping a note of what you have achieved in your diary.

WHAT'S IMPORTANT TO YOU? CHECKING YOUR VALUES

We have discussed in an earlier chapter how doctors and managers will share many values as expressed, for example, in the General Medical Council's (GMC's) ethical code 'Good Medical Practice' [2]. In fact, it goes wider than that. Martin Seligman, known to psychiatrists for developing the 'learned helplessness' model of depression and subsequent work on 'learned optimism' later developed an interest in 'positive psychology' [3]. A typology of human values and virtues that reflected an 'ideal' state of human functioning (character strengths) was developed. This was based on an overview of cultures, philosophies and religions in an attempt to discover values that were universally (or at least very widely) held in high esteem by different cultures. Twenty-four specific strengths consistently emerged across history and cultures under six broad headings: wisdom, courage, humanity, justice, temperance, and transcendence. These are expanded in Box 4.1. They are important because they cause us to appreciate that the dominant values of late twentieth-century and early twenty-first-century capitalism (based on an erroneous interpretation by some economic theorists of the Darwinian doctrine of competition and 'survival of the fittest') are not the only values. There is a pervasive cynicism in modern culture that tends to attribute everything to

BOX 4.1: Modified from the Values in Action (VIA) Institute classification of human strengths (www.viacharacter.org/Classification/Classification/tabid/238/Default.aspx)

Wisdom and knowledge: Cognitive strengths

- Creativity
- Curiosity
- Judgement and open-mindedness (including thinking critically)
- Love of learning
- Perspective

Courage: Motional or *motivational* strengths involving exercise of will

- Bravery
- Perseverance
- Honesty
- Zest

Humanity: Interpersonal strengths

- Capacity to love and be loved
- Kindness
- Social intelligence (including emotional intelligence)

Justice: Civic strengths that underlying healthy community life

- Teamwork
- Fairness
- Leadership

Temperance: Strengths that protect against excess

- Forgiveness and mercy
- Modesty and humility
- Prudence
- Self-regulation

Transcendence: Strengths that forge connections and provide meaning

- Appreciation of beauty and excellence
- Gratitude
- Hope
- Humour (including playfulness!)
- Religiousness and spirituality (linked to meaning and purpose)

pseudo-Darwinian, pseudo-Freudian motives such as status through appearance, riches and celebrity to enable men and women to attract the 'best' partners. In fact, as Robert Wright has ably shown in his works *The Moral Animal* and *Nonzero* [4,5] this is a very simplistic interpretation of both *biological* and *cultural* evolution. The near-universal human strengths recognised by positive psychology are an important reminder of more realistic virtues from which more useful values can be derived. On a quite different basis, a leading neo-liberal economic theorist, Brian Griffiths, argued that markets, too, need a set of values that are independent of the market [6]. He cited, as common values needed to underpin a market economy, principles of justice or fairness, mutual respect or reciprocal regard, stewardship or trusteeship of 'God's creation' and honesty or integrity (which includes truthfulness and reliability).

The values Griffiths and others recognise as essential to a well-functioning market correspond roughly to justice, humanity, courage and transcendence in the Values in Action Institute's list in Box 4.1. Interestingly, the values of temperance and wisdom do not appear in Griffiths' list. Perhaps they should and perhaps, if they did, we could have avoided the market collapse of 2008. This is a practical book, so enough of the values that motivate people; *but* they *are* important and foundational to worthwhile human achievement. Be clear about your own and those of people you have to deal with.

Conflicts of interest

With the increased use of privatised services within the NHS, there is an increased possibility of conflict of interest. Consultants and general practitioners with a financial interest in private healthcare organisations should be careful to avoid financial conflicts of interest.

MAKING DECISIONS

Doctors are used to making decisions with patients about health, illness and treatment options. They are trained to make decisions rationally and easily as part of their everyday work. The process of decision-making in a medical consultation appears relatively straightforward (see Figure 4.2).

In this model, good decisions again depend on good relationships (to gather information and build confidence) and shared values (to ensure the doctor is not imposing his or her values on the patient). This roughly corresponds to [7] *interpretive* or *deliberative* models (see Chapter 3). We all know that the reality is more complicated than this simple model would suggest. For example, information from caregivers and others may not be available. The unconscious patient is not able to convey any information (here Emanuel and Emanuel's *paternalistic* model may be more appropriate). The thoroughness of physical and mental state examination will depend upon several factors, including the physical setting and the time available. Investigations available may also

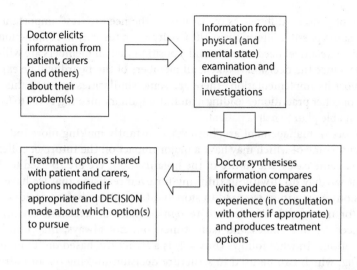

Figure 4.2 A simplified model of decision-making in a medical consultation.

be limited by local factors. The doctor's ability to synthesise information and compare it with the knowledge base will depend on experience, time, decision–support systems and other factors. Finally, the decision itself may be biased by some factor that has not been taken into account. Perhaps the best treatment option requires a service or medication that is not available (perhaps for reasons of cost), or more time than the patient can spare, or requires giving up some addictive behaviour ... and so on.

We also know that busy doctors working under pressure take 'shortcuts'. They recognise certain patterns of movement or behaviour and form diagnostic hypotheses as soon as they see the patient. They then proceed to look for evidence to verify the hypothesis. The benefit of this process is that it is often surprisingly accurate and may account for the value doctors put on lots of experience in training and beyond. The danger is that only information that supports the hypothesis is noticed; contrary information may be ignored (confirmation bias) and alternative hypotheses missed.

Collective and individual decisions

In management, decisions often appear to be taken collectively (or not at all!). In truth, decisions are often made by an individual but with the benefit of the advice and support of others. At Board level, decisions on important matters are often taken only after extensive discussion, exploration and consultation. In the discussion phase, different Board members may take opposing points of view, either because of genuine differences or because of the need to 'test' important decisions against possible alternatives. The Chairperson (usually in conjunction with the Chief Executive) needs then to find a position that all members are willing to support. Once the decision is taken, all members of the Board will be expected to support its implementation. There are some similarities between this and a doctor or other practitioner leading a multidisciplinary meeting to try to find the best available plan to help a patient.

Doctors in management are, however, constantly making more individual decisions, some of which may have a major impact on the future of colleagues or, in extreme cases, the future of the organisation. We are so used to deciding that we may do it without thinking (or even realising that we have made a decision). Sometimes we need to stop and take advice before deciding what to do (or not to do). We need to recognise that our decisions are strongly influenced by our values and (sometimes, but not always, inappropriately) our emotions. In what follows (Box 4.2) is a structure, based on [8] model for coaching, which can be used to structure decision-making on an individual or a collective basis.

BOX 4.2: John Whitmore's coaching model [8] modified as a decision-making tool

Goal: What is the purpose of this decision (or this meeting)? What outcomes are desired?

Reality: What factors are relevant in this decision? Who else is affected? What are their views (and emotional investment)? How important is this decision to you, to them, to the organisation? What are the relevant values? What are the time constraints? How much priority does this decision have? Are there any stakeholders who should/must be consulted? What resources will be necessary to support the decision and how can they be made available? Are there likely to be any obstacles and how can they be overcome?

Options: What are the different options for this decision? Can they be expanded by bringing in other factors? (See section on negotiation in Chapter 5.) What are the advantages and disadvantages of each option? Which decision is likely to deliver the best outcomes?

Will: What is your decision? To what extent does this meet all your objectives? How will you check whether it has achieved the desired outcomes? What other decisions need to be taken to put this into effect and who will be responsible for carrying them through? (Make sure they are informed and empowered – see also section on delegation in Chapter 2.)

There are two other factors vital to good decision-making. They are

1. Proportionality
2. Appropriate authority

Proportionality is obvious. For example, we hope nobody would use a tool like that in Box 4.2 when asked if they wanted a cup of tea! Most management decisions do, however, demand a degree of reflection. *'If you always do what you always did, you'll always get what you always got'* is a wise aphorism.

In coaching, a distinction is made between 'reacting' and 'responding'. Reactive decisions over important matters should be avoided. Even in emergency situations, reflection can be life-saving. Jonah Lehrer in his interesting work *The Decisive Moment* describes a situation in which a fire crew were trapped before a rapidly advancing scrub fire [9]. Most of the crew kept running and were overtaken and consumed by the fire. One, realising he was not going to outrun the fire, stopped, deliberately lit a small fire around himself to burn all the combustible material in the immediate locality and then lay down, allowing the main fire to pass around him. He survived, and his practice became a standard part of training for fire crew. The overcoming of his natural tendency for flight and some very quick thinking saved this man's life. The priority and degree of deliberation (not necessarily the length of time) we give to a decision must be proportional to the importance of that decision.

Appropriate authority is less obvious but equally vital to effective decision-making. It is no good spending a great deal of time and trouble to come to a correct decision if it is actually somebody else's to make. In the clinical situation, it is of critical importance that the decision-maker has the appropriate competences to make the decision. It is a waste of time if decisions are referred to someone who is too senior, and risky if they are made by someone too junior. Though management decisions rarely have the same urgency or the same immediate potential for harm as clinical decisions, the same principles apply.

DIFFICULT CHOICES – WHEN PERSONAL AND ORGANISATIONAL VALUES CLASH

As a doctor-manager you will frequently need to make decisions and choices or to share in collective decision-making and choices. We have already suggested some models for decision-making and emphasised the importance of aligning choices with purpose, vision, values and goals. But what can you do if there is an issue of forced choice? We are all familiar with these in the NHS and they are usually the outcome of economic reality and political theory and practice. The imposition of market disciplines on the NHS since the 1990s and increasing fragmentation and privatisation of services are good examples. Those who agreed with the political/economic theory behind these changes had no problem implementing decisions based on this model. Those who had reservations had a difficult decision: Were their values and beliefs so compromised that they had to resign? Was it more important to stay in post to attempt to mitigate the possible negative effects of the new system?

In making this kind of decision many factors will play a part, including the seniority of the management position held and the views of the rest of the management team.

This theme is picked up in Chapter 6 looking at duty of care and raising concerns.

If there is a serious lack of alignment with local management, the doctor-manager must decide whether or not they are able to persuade or otherwise influence other members of the team or whether it is more consistent with their own values and integrity to step down. This is the point to discuss influencing skills.

INFLUENCING AND PERSUADING

Influencing and persuading people is an art. But it is also an evidence-based skill. Cialdini [10] described six universal principles of social influence (Box 4.3). These are based on social psychology research and, although there is some overlap between them, they have an immediate face validity to students of human behaviour. They are also consistent with ideas of reciprocal altruism, based on evolutionary psychology [4].

Reciprocation is tied in with a basic human tendency to appreciate 'fair play'. If someone has done something for us, we feel obliged to do something for them. Being generous to others predisposes them to be generous to us. In practical terms this means being prepared to do things to support other people when they need our support. A doctor who has 'covered' my on-call at short notice is *more likely*, other things being equal, to receive a sympathetic response if she asks me for 'cover' at short notice. In many ways this is simply a restatement of the ancient principle of 'do unto others as you wish that they would do unto you'.

BOX 4.3: Cialdini's six principles of social influence

1. *Reciprocation*: We feel obliged to return favours.
2. *Authority*: We look to (trusted) experts, authorities and role models to show the way.
3. *Consistency*: We want to act consistently with our public commitments and values.
4. *Scarcity*: The less available something is, the more we tend to want it.
5. *Liking*: The more we like people, the more we want to agree with them.
6. *Social proof*: We look to others to guide our behaviour.

Source: Cialdini, R., *Influence: The Psychology of Persuasion*, Collins Business, London, UK, 2007.

The role of *authority* is to some extent diminishing in an egalitarian age, but we should not underestimate how far people will tend to follow us if they trust our authority and regard us as reliable. To be trusted authorities we need both to be seen to be competent in the area we are to be trusted in and to act with integrity and consistency. It takes time to build this kind of authority as a manager. If we have a reputation for clear thinking, effective communication and wise choices in other fields (eg as clinicians) this may give us a head start. But 'nothing succeeds like success' and people will often wait a while before deciding whether they can trust a new medical manager and whether he or she has carried over useful skills and attitudes from the clinical situation.

Because of the way doctors view other doctors, many medical managers find that this trust is better maintained if they retain a clinical input into the service. So, continuing in *effective* clinical practice is often seen as a useful way for senior medical managers to maintain their authority and credibility (at least as far as other doctors are concerned). It is worth considering how the different management cultures discussed in the last chapter understand authority. The authority of the 'club culture' derives from connectedness, that of the role culture from organisational position and that of the team culture from knowledge and skills that are useful in addressing the issues the team is tackling. The craft culture likes to be judged by the quality of its work and is sceptical of organisational authority except in the 'master–apprentice' relationship.

Those we seek to influence will have an investment in their own *consistency*. They will tend to stick to their own values, principles and allegiances. Consistency should not just be surface 'spin'. It has many aspects in common with the qualities of *congruence* and *integrity* identified as important in successful counselling and coaching relationships (and as part of the VIA set discussed earlier – Box 4.1). For many reasons it is worth involving one's clinical colleagues in aspects of management and seeking to establish genuinely shared values and principles. If colleagues have learned to be helpful in small matters, they will generally be consistent in their helpfulness when larger problems occur. Where there is a tension between beliefs, values and principles on the one hand and behaviours on the other (cognitive dissonance) this creates discomfort. To reduce this discomfort people will generally moderate their behaviour.

Therefore, it is important to get active 'sign up' to new ideas or projects from those we want to participate. Once someone has made such a commitment, they are more likely to find reasons to support the initiative. Conversely, if they are being passively dragged along or acting against their better judgement, they are more likely to resist change.

Scarcity is the basis of the science of economics. If something is rare or hard to achieve, then it is generally more highly valued and wanted. In getting people to sign up to new ways of doing things, it is good to be able to stress what is uniquely desirable about a particular approach. This often means trying to generate new ideas locally rather than blindly following national policy. One of the virtues of the Virginia Mason Production System (an adaptation for healthcare of Toyota's lean management, see Chapter 8) is that it creates a system for continuous locally driven improvement of clinical processes. Let us be the ones to show how this or that policy can be implemented *really* effectively locally. Being the best has 'scarcity value', so it is a great thing to aim for. However, in the present system of commissioning in the English NHS, commissioners sometimes tend to be wary of 'excellence', afraid that it will cost more than services that are barely adequate.

Being liked is something that many of us 'go for' naturally. Being liked and respected is a good foundation for influencing people. We are not thinking here of the 'compulsively' nice person who makes themselves into a doormat for others to tread on. Rather we are thinking of the genuine feelings of affection and mutual respect that people working together to a common cause can achieve. If being genuinely liked helps us influence people, being obnoxious, disliked and not trusted has the opposite effect. It is worth spending time building good quality genuine relationships, not just for their own sake but also for the very practical reason that they will help us when we have to influence or persuade people.

We all like to think of ourselves as independent-minded, especially in Western cultures. However, to a large extent we are validated by the 'norms' of society around us. This desire for *social proof* can produce undesirable as well as desirable behaviour! When we are trying to persuade people to change, it helps if we can cite genuine examples of others who have made and benefited from similar changes. Sometimes a successful development elsewhere can be used as a model for new developments, sometimes a local pilot scheme, properly conducted and evaluated, can be persuasive.

EXERCISE 4.2

Influencing people

Consider an area where you need to influence people. Be as specific as you can. It may be anything from the adoption of a new assessment form to a radical re-organisation of the service. Decide who the key people you need to influence are. For each person make an inventory from the points in Table 4.1 and think through your answers. Use the answers to decide how you approach those you need to influence on this and future occasions.

If you want to maximise your potential to influence other people, you should take careful note of Cialdini's principles and you may wish to read his later work [11]. We also need to have confidence in ourselves. Confidence comes with practice, recognising and celebrating success and learning from mistakes. By accelerating this process of celebrating success and learning from mistakes, coaching and mentoring (see Chapter 5) may be used to accelerate development of self-confidence and capacity to influence others.

Table 4.1 Strengthening your position when you need to influence people

Key point	Question	Answer
Reciprocation	With respect to this issue, does this person already feel that I am helpful in taking forward their issues?	
Authority	How does this person view authority and where do they think my authority in this particular area derives from?	
Consistency	How can I present the issue in a way that is consistent with his or her (hopefully shared) values and their commitments?	
Scarcity	Is there some unique benefit for the individual or group in taking this forward? What is it?	
Liking	Does this person like me?	
Social proof	Are there examples I can give where others have already made similar changes with enthusiasm and success? Will this person be impressed by these examples?	

CONCLUSIONS

Not everything is a resigning issue and certainly anyone who resigned every time he or she had to compromise would not last long in a modern health service. Disagreements need to be resolved and we should always try to be part of the solution. Compromises need to be made all the time and collective decisions upheld. It is important, however, to remember that we all have 'red lines', and where decisions transgress our fundamental values and impeach our integrity, we may have to take a stand and resign. Here, doctor-managers are fortunate. If they have negotiated their contracts carefully and kept up to date clinically, they always have the option of reverting to full-time clinical (or clinical and academic) work.

REFERENCES

1. Covey SR (2016) *The 7 Habits of Highly Effective People*. New York: Simon and Schuster. FranklinCovey, Mango Media Inc. (Kindle Edition).
2. General Medical Council (2013) *Good Medical Practice*. London, UK: GMC. http://www.gmc-uk.org/guidance/good_medical_practice.asp (accessed 30 April 2018).

3. Seligman M (2003) *Authentic Happiness*. London, UK: Nicholas Brealey.
4. Wright R (1994) *The Moral Animal*. London, UK: Abacus.
5. Wright R (2001) *Nonzero*. London, UK: Abacus.
6. Griffiths B (1982) *Morality and the Marketplace*. London, UK: Hodder and Stoughton.
7. Emanuel E and Emanuel L (1992) Four models of the physician-patient relationship. *The Journal of the American Medical Association*, 267(16): 2221–2229.
8. Whitmore J (2017) *Coaching for Performance*, 5th ed. London, UK: Nicholas Brealey.
9. Lehrer J (2009) *The Decisive Moment*. Edinburgh, UK: Canongate Books.
10. Cialdini R (2007) *Influence: The Psychology of Persuasion*. London, UK: Collins Business.
11. Cialdini R (2017) *Pre-Suasion: A Revolutionary Way to Influence and Persuade*. London, UK: Random House Books.

FURTHER READING

Morton C (2003) *By the Skin of Our Teeth*. London, UK: Middlesex University Press.

5

People skills

This chapter is based on the premise that everyone needs to develop skills to be able to function within the complex and diverse groups that exist in healthcare settings. The ability to work flexibly and responsively with the people we encounter needs developing. Acquiring these skills is not an exact science. We know that people respond well to authenticity and badly to jargon and 'management-speak'. However, when you are in a pressurised situation with peers or patients, a key skill is that of self-regulation and being able to contain your own and other people's anxieties. Finding ways of relating to others that you are comfortable with and balancing all the different pressures requires practice, so we have included in this section several exercises and activities that you can try in your workplace.

COMMUNICATION

Poor communication is often given as the reason for failure. 'Our policies were correct, but we communicated them badly' is a phrase often repeated by politicians and some senior managers. BP senior management say they were trying to communicate the importance of safety across the organisation in 2010 when the *Deepwater Horizon* oil spill occurred in the Gulf of Mexico. Toyota (more about them later) were seeking to communicate the 'Toyota production method' (and culture) in rapidly expanding international manufacturing plants when they were hit by scandals about faulty accelerator and braking systems. So, what is the essence of communication?

Remember the equation from Chapter 1:

$$\text{Communication} \sim \text{trust} = \text{character} \times \text{competence}$$

In order to 'receive' a communication, we have to trust the source in terms of both character and competence. There are other factors, too, including the following:

- Communication is essentially two-way (or multilateral)
- What is said must match what is done (or trust is eroded)

- Particular communication skills are needed to deal with authoritarian or bullying cultures ('toxic workplace dynamics')
- The form of communication must suit the situation

COMMUNICATION IS ESSENTIALLY TWO-WAY (OR MULTILATERAL)

Stephen Covey [1] puts this succinctly in one of his Seven Habits: listen *and* be heard. Just as if we wish to influence people, we need to reciprocate, so if we want people to listen to us, we must listen to them. Doctors and others in the helping professions are taught the skills of empathetic listening. Simply reflecting back the content and emotional tone of what others tell us is a remarkably powerful way of making them feel valued and encouraging them to tell us even more. When, dealing with difficult or suspicious patients, doctors are often advised to abandon the traditional medical interrogation of the patient and switch to empathetic listening as the most effective way of eliciting information. But in management terms, listening is not enough. We must also be able to make our own ideas heard.

Another idea from coaching is valuable here. It is the distinction between reacting and responding. When we are in conversation, we often react with our own ideas to what the other person is saying without properly listening to them. A better way is to listen attentively, pause if necessary to consider how their point of view relates to (and perhaps modifies) our own, then give our point of view. Without this consideration of the other person's point of view, there is no possibility of a creative synthesis of ideas occurring. Whilst some doctors are too certain that their own point of view is the right one, others (including some doctors in management) are too diffident. We should value our own ideas and seek to create a listening climate in which all points of view can be heard and considered respectfully.

WHAT IS SAID MUST MATCH WHAT IS DONE

Human beings have very powerful hypocrisy detectors. If what is said does not match what is done, we usually spot this very quickly. The failure may be due to insincerity, poor management or uncontrollable external circumstances; but the dissonance will be noted and likely attributed to insincerity or incompetence, whatever the real reason. Again, this can be understood in evolutionary terms as one of the consequences and conditions of reciprocal altruism. This means that it is very important for any doctor in management to be prepared to deliver what they declare! Sometimes, a failure to deliver will be excused because colleagues understand that unpredictable external events beyond a manager's control are responsible. Some coaches use the aphorism 'under-promise, over-deliver' which emphasises the importance of not undertaking to do something we do not subsequently achieve. This is particularly the case if you are dealing with an issue of conflict at work such as a case of bullying or victimisation. When something has gone wrong, it is important to both acknowledge that something has gone wrong and also to acknowledge what steps you are going to take to remedy them. People are very rarely satisfied with kind words and cheering up – when something has gone wrong, it is important to act.

TACKLING TOXIC WORKPLACE DYNAMICS

Sadly, many people working in the NHS experience bullying and harassment. When ignored, this has a powerfully corrosive effect on working relationships. Being ignored when concerns or positive ideas are raised is also harmful and disrespectful, leading to people feeling undervalued. Of course, it is best to avoid a bullying culture and develop mutually respectful relationships at work. Valuing people and the contribution they make to the organisation produces better results. Creating conditions where employees are 'engaged' and respected improves staff satisfaction and retention. However, it is also important to know what to do when things go wrong; bullying or harassment should never be ignored, and it pays to be aware of the legal responsibilities of employers in this regard. Harassment as a form of discrimination is unlawful – enshrined in the Equality Act 2010 (see Box 5.1) – and, although there is no specific legislation against bullying, there are anti-discrimination laws and policies which identify disability, sexuality, religion or belief, class, age, gender and race as potential bases of discrimination. In addition, employers have a legal duty to protect the health, including mental health, and safety of workers whether directly employed or not.

BOX 5.1: Legal responsibilities of employers

- Employers have a duty to prevent harassment, bullying and discrimination at work.
- Staff are covered by anti-discrimination law from day one of employment.
- Staff must be protected against victimisation for raising a complaint.
- Staff can bring complaints under laws covering discrimination and harassment, health and safety and unfair dismissal.
- The 'protected characteristics' in The Equality Act 2010 are gender, pregnancy and maternity, race, disability, sexual orientation, age, gender reassignment, marriage and civil partnership, and religion or belief.

BOX 5.2: Letter of concerns

Dear.............................

I am writing to complain about what you (did/said) to me (on date/ yesterday/this morning) when you...
....

Over the (time period)..... you have...................................
I want you to stop this behaviour...................................
I find this offensive and unacceptable. I am keeping a copy of this letter and I shall take further action if you do not stop immediately.
Yours sincerely,

The first step in addressing discrimination could be to put in writing your concerns to the person involved (Box 5.2).

There is a lot of literature about bullying at work, a sad reflection of how widespread it is. As part of employers' responsibilities to protect people from bullying, the following actions can be considered:

- The bully is transferred to another section or another department on the same site, or to another branch of the organisation.
- Until further notice, any attempt by the bully to make direct contact with previous colleagues, other than through an appointed third person, will result in disciplinary measures.
- The bully is made fully aware of the effect their behaviour has been having on others.
- The bully is removed from any position of managing other employees until their behaviours have been addressed.

Taking a case to law is generally considered to be the last resort when everything else has failed. There is a nationally set 'three-step' procedure for dealing with dismissal, discipline and grievance issues which must be followed before a legal case can be taken. They are:

- Completing a statement in writing outlining the grounds for grievance
- Carrying out a meeting between the parties involved
- Carrying out an appeal if requested after this meeting

If the grievance process fails, then the employee can make a claim to an employment tribunal within a 3-month period. There are three grounds for such an appeal:

- Unfair dismissal
- Discrimination
- Unfair deductions from pay

THE FORM OF COMMUNICATION MUST SUIT THE SITUATION

Communicating with the media is very different from communicating with patients, with colleagues or with managers from other disciplines. Respect for the other party is essential in all cases, but in other ways, different considerations apply in terms of the following:

1. *Purpose of communication*
   - Courts
   - Disciplinary
   - Public
   - Patients and carers
   - Media
2. *Language* (not just English or other languages but also the appropriateness to the situation in terms of complexity and use of technical terms, acronyms and so on)
3. *Timing*

Doctors appearing in court

Appearing in court also requires special training to deal with potentially challenging questioning from solicitors or barristers. If they are witnesses to fact, they should stick to the simple truth. If they are 'expert' witnesses, they should beware of straying outside their field of competence and be humble enough to answer 'I don't know' if they don't. Similar considerations apply in quasi-legal proceedings like disciplinary hearings.

Communicating with the public

This is often part of the medical manager's job, particularly when there is consultation over planned service changes. In this case there will usually be a communication strategy worked out by specialists in the organisation. This will usually involve several approaches including public meetings and a strategy for communicating via local media. It is important that clinicians in the organisation have an appropriate level of input into such consultations. This means that they need to be involved in planning the changes from the beginning as well as in contributing to any public consultation. Service changes are often resisted, even when they are moving the service in a positive direction. Resistance is likely to be even stronger when the primary reason for changes is cutting expenditure. Nevertheless, this is sometimes necessary and medical managers must take their part even (or perhaps especially) in controversial consultations.

Communicating with patients and caregivers

This is part of every doctor's job. Here the use of understandable (not patronising) language, the recognition that, in highly emotional situations, communication may have to be repeated and the value of written information are all important considerations. The medical manager is more likely to be involved in communication with patients or relatives if there has been a serious untoward incident or a complaint. Here a genuinely sympathetic attitude is vital, coupled with a rigorous respect for the truth and recognition that how people perceive a situation depends on where they stand. Every effort should be made to communicate in an adult manner and to avoid 'crossed transactions', in transactional analysis (TA) terms (see Chapter 2). Timing is important too. As discussed earlier, a positive and open attitude to dealing informally with questions and complaints at the time they arise may often avoid a more formal complaint being made, involving a great deal of time, investigation and often misery for all concerned. Where there is a formal complaint, any investigation and communication of the outcome should be as rapid as possible so that complainants are not kept waiting unnecessarily. When delays are inevitable because of the need to investigate complicated situations or because of the need to conduct legal and/or disciplinary inquiries without prejudice, then complainants should be kept as fully informed as possible about the delays and the reasons for them. Most healthcare organisations will have staff who specialise in managing complaints and will draw in help from medical managers, human resources departments and other doctors when necessary. The complaints staff should also have detailed knowledge of local procedures, timelines and the recording of investigations. They are important allies in supporting medical managers and all those dealing with complaints.

Doctors dealing with the media

Doctors in this role should have special training. This is often a role that falls to doctors in management, especially Medical Directors. One of the authors remembers attending a media training weekend where a very senior psychiatrist was 'taken apart' in a mock 'hostile interview' by an even more prominent radio journalist. Every media interview should be considered as potentially hostile and the interviewee should go into the interview with a clear idea of the (usually up to three) points they wish to communicate and a determination to give straight answers to reasonable questions. Unreasonable, leading questions designed to show the doctor or his organisation up in a bad light should be firmly, calmly and politely refused or deflected.

THE SPECIAL CASE OF EMAIL (AND OTHER FORMS OF E-COMMUNICATION, INCLUDING TEXT MESSAGING)

What we have written so far applies mainly to verbal communication, though the same principles apply for written communication. However, nothing about modern communication could be complete without a brief word on the 'splendours and miseries' of e-communication. Table 5.1 lists some of the benefits and pitfalls of e-communication.

One of our colleagues used to say that if she ever reacted to a situation by writing an angry letter she would put it to one side for a day or two and possibly get

Table 5.1 Benefits and pitfalls of email and other e-communication

Benefits	Pitfalls
Fast	Fast
Cost-effective (apparently)	Information overload (meaning important messages may be overlooked and recipients may be stressed trying to process it all), which can be anything but cost-effective
A 'written record', easy to broadcast, can be used in the courts	A 'written record', easy to broadcast (and copy) leading to over-involvement of people in matters that are not important to them and a potential risk in litigation; risks to confidentiality
Asynchronous	Easy to write and react without due consideration and to pass problems on inappropriately
Informal	Easily misunderstood
'In the moment'	(Potentially) preserved forever!

a respected colleague to read it before it was sent. Nine times out of ten the letter would not be sent or would be heavily modified before it went out. The problem with e-communication is that it is possible to get one's thoughts to other people rather too quickly. Much better to reflect and consult before sending or reacting to an angry email. Because emails do not convey emotional tone in the same way as a face-to-face or telephone conversation, misunderstandings can sometimes happen, with something intended as a 'joke' being perceived as offensive. Generally, confidential information should not be sent by email unless appropriate encryption is used.

Some organisations have policies to reduce information overload, for example, by restricting those who can authorise emails with wide circulation. An ideal situation is to have a trusted, reliable and efficient personal assistant with sufficient time to sort incoming emails on behalf of the manager and prioritise them, even deleting those which are clearly irrelevant. Having physician assistants to do this (amongst many other tasks) was one of the ways the Virginia Mason Production System (Chapter 8) improved the efficiency of their primary care physicians [2]. In any case, one has to become ruthless in dealing with that which is unimportant but (appears) urgent simply because it appears in the inbox. For more consideration of issues of urgency and importance, see the section 'Time management'.

NEGOTIATING

Negotiating skills are often identified as a deficit by doctors new to management. In fact, it is relatively unusual for doctors in management to be directly involved in formal negotiations. Though they will often contribute to negotiations, for example, between commissioners and providers of service, their role will usually be more as technical advisors rather than as direct negotiators. Nevertheless, a sound understanding of the principles of negotiation is often very useful in less formal settings. For example, a 'job planning interview' with a consultant is essentially a negotiation and many of our conversations with our colleagues, patients and families and carers have elements of negotiation in them.

The authors of *Getting to 'Yes'* [3], who were themselves part of a major project on negotiation at Harvard University, were involved in real-life negotiations in many contexts. Their text speaks from experience, not just theory. They make a vital distinction between *positional* and *principled* negotiation. Positional negotiation is common in everyday life. People take positions (often somewhat extreme) and barter their way to a compromise. Some negotiators are 'hard' in their approach; others are 'soft'. Hard negotiators will often seem to do well but often at the expense of damaging long-term relationships and storing up problems for the future. There are many other reasons why positional bargaining is often inefficient and ineffective. The main points of principled negotiation are summed up in Box 5.3.

Separating the people from the problem means working hard not to see our partners in negotiation as 'the other side' or, worse still, 'the enemy'. They are real people too, with their own ambitions, emotions and the agenda of those they represent on their shoulders. The ideal position is to establish a genuine partnership in solving problems for the common benefit.

Concentrating on interests, not positions, facilitates this approach of mutual respect. It is worth trying to find out what the real interests are of any party with whom you are negotiating. Focusing on interests rather than positions makes it easier to satisfy the needs of both parties. Take time to find out what the other parties to a negotiation really want. Make sure they understand what you want, not in terms of a fixed position but in terms of what would really satisfy you or those you represent.

If you know what interests the other party wishes to satisfy and they know what you want, it is much easier to work together to come up with options. At this stage it is useful to broaden the focus. Are there other factors that can be brought into the situation that will enable more potentially satisfying options to be designed? There should be no premature commitment to any particular option. At this stage all parties should be clear that they are generating ideas, not committing to positions. From these ideas, more new ideas may spring.

BOX 5.3: The main points of *principled negotiation*

- Separate the *people* from the *problem*.
- Focus on *interests* not *positions*.
- Invent *options* for *mutual* gain.
- Insist on *objective* criteria.

Source: [3].

When it comes to choosing between options, it is best to agree on objective criteria for judging between them. Hopefully it then becomes relatively easy to find one or more options that leave all parties satisfied with the outcome. This is a very brief description of the main points in *principled negotiation*. Fisher et al. [3] go into each area in considerably more depth and anybody who is likely to be involved personally in negotiation should read their work.

EXAMPLE 5.1: Negotiating before taking on extra leadership responsibility

A Trust wants a high-performing Consultant to take on extra leadership and management responsibilities. The Trust offers to pay up to two additional sessions in recognition of the extra work. However, the Consultant is, in reality, already working a 48-hour week and does not want to extend her hours further. She examines the workload of other doctors in the service and finds that an Associate Specialist whose clinical judgement she trusts is about to come to the end of a specially funded project working with asylum-seekers 1 day each week. She discusses matters with him and proposes that he take on her clinics and provide emergency cover for her patients for a full day each week. She suggests to the Trust that she would be happy to take the equivalent of one extra session as a (superannuable) 'special responsibility payment'. She suggests that the other session they would have paid her can help resolve the problem of keeping the Associate Specialist on a full-time contract now that the source of short-term funding has come to an end. The Trust agrees.

EXERCISE 5.1
Negotiating an agreement

Consider an area where you have had to negotiate about funding, pay, medical cover or one of many other possible areas. Was the negotiation conducted as a confrontation between different 'positions' or on a 'principled' basis? Did you follow the guidelines listed in Box 5.3? Did you do the following?

- Separate the *people* from the *problem*.
- Focus on *interests* not *positions*.
- Invent *options* for mutual gain.
- Insist on *objective* criteria.

How could you have improved your approach to the negotiation? How will you behave differently next time? Try using these principles the next time you are involved in a negotiation.

In this example, all involved have focused on interests rather than positions. It is in the Trust's interest to have a doctor working in management and leadership who has genuinely got 'protected' time to devote to this work. By spending less on the Consultant's management responsibilities, they also find money to help ease the situation of employing the Associate Specialist 5 days a week despite the loss of 1 day's special funding. It is in the Consultant's interest not to be overworked and to have a protected day for her management work. It is in the Associate Specialist's interest to have new work to replace a short-term project coming to a natural end. Consider also how the Consultant has demonstrated her knowledge of the service and suitability for her new role by widening options and finding a new role for the Associate Specialist 1 day per week at minimal cost to the Trust. Finally, her proposal to take the extra money as a special responsibility allowance reflects reality and ensures that her pension fund is better than it would otherwise have been.

COOPERATIVE WORKING: COMPLEXITY DEMANDS CO-OPERATION

Consider how complicated the world has become and how much the practice of medicine has changed in the last 50 years. The oldest of the authors was taught in medical school by clinicians who had qualified and practiced in the pre-antibiotic era. Pagers ('bleeps') were a recent innovation. Specialist Coronary Care Units were being developed and total hip replacements were a novelty. Computed Tomography (CT) scans, Nuclear Magnetic Resonance Imaging (NMRI) and numerous other investigatory tools were still a thing of the future and the choice of drugs was extremely limited compared with today's pharmacopoeia.

This was just as well since, in the absence of easy access to ready reference tables, interactions between drugs largely had to be memorised. Spending on health was relatively low and the authority of doctors was largely unchallenged.

Now the sheer complexity of the health system demands good management and a culture of co-operation. There is a tendency to 'tribalism' in human nature that sets the interests of our own group against those of other groups. It probably evolved at a time when it significantly enhanced chances of survival. Two of the authors belong to the 'tribe' of old-age psychiatry (and perhaps to the tribes of academia and management as well) and often see that specialty as under-resourced and 'missing out' when special funding comes along. You may belong to the 'tribe' of oncologists, cardiologists, general practitioners, gastroenterologists or one of many others. If you are a medical manager with wider responsibilities, you have to put aside your feeling of loyalty to your specialty of origin or, perhaps better, you need to develop equivalent loyalty to other areas.

Of course, competition is important, too. Politicians sometimes see it as the only way to 'drive change'. This viewpoint is based on the assumption that all who disagree with a particular political theory are curmudgeonly stick-in-the-muds who will resist change. In fact, often services only survive because of the flexibility and co-operation of those who do the work with patients. Friendly competition may well be a way of improving standards (eg in clinical audit), but hostile competition is another matter and can be destructive. In our view it has little place in a well-run healthcare system.

ITERATION: MUTUAL UNDERSTANDING, INTEREST AND ENGAGEMENT

Iteration literally means travelling or journeying. In management it reflects the principle that managers should not be 'out of touch' with the parts of the organisation that deliver and support the core business. Sometimes the Boards of organisations will meet on different sites and spend time meeting the workforce and discussing important matters with them. Sometimes individual Directors will take an interest in particular functional or geographical units of the service. Senior medical managers need to keep in touch with the work their medical colleagues are involved in. They can do this partly through meetings, but these should be supplemented by visits where a proper balance is achieved between informality and reality. We need to avoid the situation where board members either get too optimistic a picture (often when formal presentations are made to them) or too pessimistic a picture (often when someone 'with an axe to grind' overstates problems in the hope of prompting a solution). If the organisation has a culture of honest communication, it will be relatively easy to avoid these extremes.

Part of the purpose of iteration is to enable managers to get an accurate picture of the services they manage. Part of the purpose is to develop mutual understanding so that managers appreciate the pressures and complexities of clinical reality and clinicians appreciate the pressures on managers. Medical managers are particularly well placed to promote this mutual understanding as they 'have a foot in both camps'. Finally, iteration can promote engagement. Clinicians (and support service managers) may, once they engage with the realities faced by senior management, be able to offer solutions at no or low cost. Similarly, senior managers, when they understand the problems faced by clinicians and support service managers, may be able to broker solutions, perhaps by small organisational changes (eg making patient record/computing staff relate more directly to clinicians). Innovative ways of achieving this co-operative culture are discussed in Chapter 8.

> **EXERCISE 5.2**
> **Understanding performance**
>
> Whatever the level of your management job, consider what steps you need to take to become familiar with the issues facing those you manage (and those who manage you). There are of course many ways of becoming familiar with other people's points of view: listening in meetings, having 'one-to-one' conversations, keeping in touch electronically and so on. But here we are literally concerned with steps – that is physically moving into their situation and perhaps discussing issues face to face in that situation. If you don't do this already, consider whether you might and decide what item of lower priority in your timetable might need to be given less time in order to make the process of iteration a reality.

DEVELOPING OTHERS

One of the tasks of any professional is to help develop future and junior members of that profession. For doctors, this often means being involved in the education and supervision of medical students and doctors in training. For medical managers, there is also an imperative to develop the management capability and capacity of their doctor colleagues (if only so that they can stand down with an assurance that there is someone competent to take over in due course). All doctors are, to some extent, involved in management and senior medical managers can develop colleagues' competences in this area by a variety of means. Delegation has been discussed previously. If colleagues have areas they passionately want to develop (provided the areas are appropriate and acceptable to the organisation), then it is worth giving them support to develop a business case for the development and, if the service commissioner or other organisation agrees to fund the development, helping them develop and manage the implementation of a business plan and project plan to take the development forward. This introduces them to the realities of getting a project funded and of carrying it through to completion. NAViGO, a social enterprise described in Case Study 4.1 and Chapter 8, was strengthened by consultants each having their own area to develop and thus extra and needed services (including a borderline personality disorder service, a family therapy group and a service for people with eating disorders) were provided at minimal cost to the organisation.

Feedback from colleagues and 360-degree feedback, if properly managed as part of the appraisal/job planning/personal development cycle, is another way of encouraging development of management and leadership skills. This process can also lead to the identification of areas for further development that can be addressed in other ways including the following:

- Courses
- Learning sets and management clubs
- Coaching and mentoring

Further development for medical mangers is discussed in more detail in Chapter 10.

COURSES

Management and leadership courses come in many varieties. Sometimes they can be excellent, sometimes they feel like a waste of time and money and sometimes they *are* a waste of time and money! Day release or half-day release courses run by reputable universities and leading to diplomas or even Master's degrees in management and leadership can be very valuable for someone new to a senior management post. The NHS Leadership Academy [4] offers a variety of courses. Short courses, sometimes run on-site, by training organisations can introduce whole groups of doctors to useful concepts. However, it is often difficult to judge the quality of such courses in advance. Perhaps the best way of finding whether they meet local needs is to speak to others who have been on them. Distance learning with occasional 'summer schools' or weekends away is another useful way of packaging management training. Before embarking on any costly courses, it is essential to review what is available, to take advice and to count the cost to the person and the organisation in terms of time as well as money (there is more on this in Chapter 10).

LEARNING SETS AND MANAGEMENT CLUBS

Action learning sets (Box 5.4), bringing together managers at a similar stage of development, often from different organisations, to discuss and reflect on real-life management issues are valuable and often form part of wider (eg day release) courses. Management clubs more often involve managers at different levels within

---

BOX 5.4: Action learning sets

Action learning sets are a common way for people to establish reflective groups at work. Action learning involves dialogue, reflection, and collective problem-solving and is consistent with the methods and principles of emancipatory education described in this book. Within healthcare, there is some acceptance that these work-focused groups are legitimate and useful in building patient care and so are a good way to start to establish better relationships at work.

PRINCIPLES AND PRACTICES
The groups are set up to run according to a set of principles:

- Confidentiality of the discussions
- Everyone is equal in the group
- Voluntary attendance but commitment to attend regularly
- Commitment made by participants to share their knowledge and experiences and to listen and learn from each other
- Commitment to collective problem-solving and planning that comes out of the group

the same organisation. They may focus on discussing particular issues and some mimic medical journal clubs by trying to find good-quality management research to inform the discussion.

How to organise an action learning set

One of the great things about action learning sets is that they can be flexible to their environment. You can run them for 1.5 hours to half a day, normally no more than 10 members approximately once or twice a month. They can be described in any way you think will work in getting people to join – from book clubs to reflective groups – use whatever language you think people will be receptive to. People tend to find it easier to attend a more technical learning set – such as discussing new policy or research – but the reality is, however you start, the key is to develop a safe and containing space for people to say what they think.

Most new groups will have a regular facilitator with some experience of workplace supervision (such as psychotherapists or other clinicians). However, it depends on the group's experience, and in health settings you often find rotating facilitation.

Meetings normally start with people doing a quick update of where they are. In health settings, it is often the case that the group will focus on one critical incident – with a short report and then an open discussion about how to understand what has occurred and what action can be taken by the team to resolve or to learn from the incident. Normally the presenter will listen to the group's reactions and then reflect on what they have learned at the end. Groups can set themes, like bullying or racism, and are expected to find collective solutions and actions to take away with them.

Groups do not have to go on forever – they often work for 6 months, after which the focus can drift. This is not a failure if relationships within the group have been strengthened. The main thing is to keep the energy and pace of the group for as long as people feel it is useful. Groups can also shift in their focus and membership – again, as long as it is responsive to what people actually want, this is a good thing. ALSs (action learning sets) work if they are useful, so the key is to respond to the needs that come up rather than to stick to the original plan (Elizabeth Cotton [5]).

COACHING AND MENTORING

These are distinct but closely related activities. Coaching is an evolving professional discipline. Coaches are trained to *support people through change, promote a balanced life, accelerate personal development and enable people to realise their potential.* Mentors will tend to be more-senior members of the same profession who support junior colleagues by discussing issues with them and sometimes intervening in the organisation on their behalf. Mentors may not have training but when they do, it will often follow similar lines to coach training but not usually in so much detail. Having emphasised the difference, it is important to realise that good mentors will often use very similar methods to coaches and that coaches who have appropriate experience will sometimes (subject to the client's agreement) explicitly move into mentoring the client, based on the coach's experience in similar situations. Coaches who do this are usually diligent in being

---

BOX 5.5: International Coach Federation core competences

1. Setting the foundation
   a. Meeting ethical guidelines and professional standards
   b. Establishing the coaching agreement
2. Co-creating the relationship
   c. Establishing trust and intimacy with the client
   d. Coaching presence
3. Communicating effectively
   e. Active listening
   f. Powerful questioning
   g. Direct communication
4. Facilitating learning and results
   h. Creating awareness
   i. Designing actions
   j. Planning and goal setting
   k. Managing progress and accountability

---

specific about the shift to mentoring and reminding the client that what worked for the coach in a similar situation may not meet the client's needs.

One of the authors is a trained coach and has taught coaching skills to doctors. What follows is a brief description, based on his experience.

The International Coach Federation (ICF; https://www.coachfederation.org/) has described 11 core competences for coaches in four groups. These are listed in Box 5.5.

Most of these are in familiar areas for doctors. Ethical guidelines and professional standards are similar to those in medicine, with bounded confidentiality and practising within the limits of one's own ability as two examples of standards shared by doctors and coaches. Co-creating the relationship bears some resemblance to what old-fashioned doctors used to call 'bedside manners'. Active listening, powerful questioning and direct communication are areas in which doctors have or should have training. However, in coaching and developmental work, generally the *purpose* of questioning is quite different from the usual purpose of questioning in medicine. Medical questioning is usually designed to elicit specific information from the patient that the doctor can use in formulating a diagnosis and treatment plan. In coaching, questions are one of several techniques used to increase the client's awareness of the situation they are in and the options they have for action. Again, the action plan should come from the client, not the coach, and responsibility for carrying it through (and any consequences of so doing) rests firmly with the client. It is this shift from the 'expert' or 'medical' model that most doctors find hard to make when learning to coach. Mentoring, being often based on having trodden the same path the mentee is now treading, does not demand such a radical shift.

As well as core competences, there are different models for structuring a coaching contract and each session. Whilst, in the opinion of the authors, it is not appropriate for those without the necessary training to set up as coaches and to offer coaching contracts, it is highly appropriate for those with the requisite skills to use coaching competences and models in helping colleagues develop *their* competences. This may be done in educational or managerial supervision, or more informally on a peer basis.

We have already discussed Whitmore's 'GROW' [6] model and how it can be applied to decision-making (see Chapter 4). When someone comes asking for help or advice on a management (or clinical) issue, a similar method can be applied. Ask their permission to use a structured tool. Then ask them 'What is your Goal with respect to this particular issue?' When this is clear, support them in exploring the Reality of the situation. When all relevant factors have been taken into account, move on to ask them to generate Options for action and to choose which option(s) they will commit to.

There are many other models and there is only space here to consider one more. This was developed by one of the authors because none of the models he could find stressed the cardinal importance of the *relationship* between coach and client. The method for planning how to achieve a vision or a goal summarised in Figure 4.1 is based upon it. Here it is again (Figure 5.1) in its original form.

In this model, the Relationship between the coach and the coachee and the 'personal foundation' of the coachee are seen as the starting point. 'Personal foundation' is a technical term from coaching that is shorthand for the level of character development of the individual. The next step is Enquiry, to find out about the situation here and now, the desired goal and the size of the gap

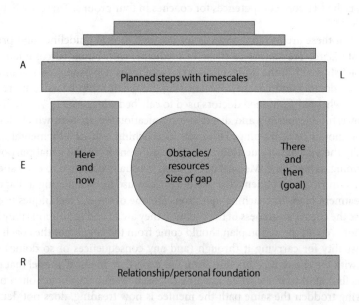

Figure 5.1 The 'REAL' model of coaching.

between them. This stage also includes a consideration of potential obstacles and resources needed and a possible trimming of the goal if it appears unrealistic. Next comes Action, chunking the task into reasonable steps with timescales, and finally Learning, when the consequences of the actions are reviewed and any necessary adjustments made. This cycle can be repeated again and again.

In this chapter so far we have discussed some important 'people' skills. They are

- Communication
- Negotiating
- Developing co-operative culture and the place of competition
- Iteration, mutual understanding, interest and engagement
- Developing others through the appraisal/job planning/personal development cycle and through courses, learning sets and coaching and mentoring

We have given extra space to coaching because we believe it is a foundational skill for a good manager (possibly for a good clinician as well) and because its competences and models can so easily be adapted to the management situation. We would also strongly suggest that any doctor new to a senior management position would be well advised to seek a good coach or mentor (possibly both). It will help to keep things in proportion and reduce stress. The final issue to discuss here is how to avoid undue stress and how to manage stressful situations when they occur (and they *do* occur). This is further developed in Chapter 9: 'When the going gets tough'.

REDUCING AND MANAGING STRESS

Stress occurs when we feel that we do not have the resources (personal or organisational) to meet targets or standards that are important to us. It is common in healthcare organisations where personal and political aspirations are rarely matched by adequate resources. One of the consequences of long-term stress is 'burnout'. In a follow-up work, Cary Cherniss published *Beyond Burnout* [7] which looked at factors that helped caring professionals prevail in adverse circumstances. These included

- Meaningful work that made a significant impact
- Intellectual stimulation
- Change
- Cultivation of special interests
- Alignment between individual and organisational needs
- Greater professional autonomy

The first four of these protective factors are (or should be) available to senior doctors in a well-run service. Alignment between individual and organisational needs has already been discussed as part of the appraisal and job-planning process and in the section on decision-making. Greater professional autonomy is an issue. Whilst senior doctors enjoy more autonomy than most professions working in modern managed healthcare systems, there seems to be constant pressure to erode autonomy through the standardisation (and in some cases the restriction) of practice. Clinical guidelines abound; some are evidence-based, many are based on a balance of scientific evidence and concerns about limiting costs. One of the jobs of medical managers is to seek to protect an appropriate degree of professional autonomy. This not only helps protect clinicians against burnout, it also enables treatment to be tailored to individual patients in individual situations. Finally, any healthcare organisation should provide appropriate support to its staff, through peer group support and, when appropriate, coaching and/or mentoring.

So much for reducing the impact of 'slow-burning' stress. What about the stress of too much work and impossible deadlines? A number of factors help here:

- Time management
- A balanced lifestyle
- Appropriate emotional detachment

TIME MANAGEMENT

Some of the best ideas in this area come from Stephen Covey and his colleagues [8]. They suggest that we look at our daily work and allocate activities on a grid that separates them into four quadrants:

1. Urgent and important
2. Not urgent but important
3. Urgent but not important
4. Not urgent and not important

Crises and projects and presentations with short deadlines come into the first quadrant. Preventative actions, strategic thinking, relationship-building and thinking about values and how they relate to current reality come in the second. Some meetings, phone calls and emails come in the third; and trivia, junk mail, some phone calls and 'escape activities' (such as playing 'spider solitaire' on the computer) come in quadrant four. It is inevitable that senior managers spend a significant part of their time in quadrant one. Even here, good planning can shift some activities into quadrant two by starting work well in advance of deadlines for example. Most people don't spend enough time in quadrant two and Covey and his colleagues argue that this is because of 'urgency addiction'. People allow urgent but unimportant matters to dominate their time budgets. Of course, they then feel so 'phased out' they waste more time in quadrant four, where computer games and the like give a spurious sense of achievement.

EXERCISE 5.3
Managing your time

Using the following grid, review a day or a week and list where you spend your working time. Try to work out what percentage of your time you spend in each quadrant. According to Covey and colleagues, workers in 'high-performance' organisations spend 20%–25% of their time in quadrant one, 65%–80% of their time in quadrant two, 15% in quadrant three and less than 1% in quadrant four. (They cite corresponding figures for 'typical' organisations as 25%–30%, 15%, 50%–60% and 2%–3%.) How do you and your organisation compare? What can you do to move yourself towards the 'high-performance' end of the spectrum?

	Urgent	Not urgent
Important	1	2
Not important	3	4

By removing some of the pressure of the urgent, good time management not only improves performance, it also reduces the stress of feeling there is never enough time to do what needs to be done.

BALANCED LIFESTYLE

This is dealt with more fully in Chapter 11. For now, it is important to say that work should never dominate our lives to the detriment of our personal relationships, our wider contribution to society and the meeting of our own legitimate needs.

APPROPRIATE EMOTIONAL DETACHMENT

A balanced lifestyle helps us to maintain an appropriate level of detachment from our work. If we only live to work, it is hard to put a proper perspective on problems in the work situation. Of course, it is frustrating if a change in economic circumstances or elected government means that an important project is cancelled. But it is not the end of the world. As we get older, most of us can look back on problems, failures or reversals that seemed catastrophic at the time. One of us clearly remembers failing to get appointed to an academic chair where he was the only candidate, but soon a visiting professorship was offered elsewhere. That led to the long, enjoyable and reasonably fruitful co-operation between two of the authors.

REFERENCES

1. Covey SR (2012) *The 7 Habits of Highly Effective People*. New York: Simon and Schuster.
2. Kenney C (2011) *Transforming Health Care*. Boca Raton, FL: CRC Press.
3. Fisher R, Ury W and Patton B (2012) *Getting to Yes*. London, UK: Random House Business.
4. NHS Leadership Academy. https://www.leadershipacademy.nhs .uk/programmes/ (accessed 18 October 2017).
5. Cotton E (2017) *Surviving Work in Healthcare: Helpful Stuff for People on the Frontline*. London, UK: Taylor & Francis Group.
6. Whitmore J (2017) *Coaching for Performance*, 5th ed. London, UK: Nicholas Brealey Publishing.
7. Cherniss C (1995) *Beyond Burnout: Helping Teachers, Nurses, Therapists and Lawyers Recover from Stress and Disillusionment*. New York: Routledge.
8. Covey S, Merrill A and Merrill R (1995) *First Things First*. London, UK: Simon & Schuster.

6

Organisation skills

INTRODUCTION

In the last chapter, we looked predominantly at people skills. Now we want to examine some organisational issues. As we do so, it will be apparent that, convenient as it is for heuristic purposes, such a distinction does not really hold water for long, so there is some overlap in the themes we try to tackle.

In this chapter we will examine the following:

- Managing and leading meetings
- Raising concerns
- Managing conflict
- Strategic thinking
- Business planning
- Financial control

MANAGING AND LEADING MEETINGS

It has been said that meetings 'take minutes and waste hours'. Yet meetings are often an important part of health service decision-making processes. Sometimes of course, setting up meetings is a way of avoiding decisions. Also, clinicians, whose main work is in *meeting the needs* of service users, often despair at the plethora of meetings managers call and their apparent inefficiency and ineffectiveness. In a modern healthcare organisation, there may also be issues of geographical spread and travelling time. Complex organisations probably do require a certain number of regular meetings. However, every attempt should be made to reduce the number and duration of meetings by eliminating unnecessary meetings and ensuring that necessary meetings are conducted effectively and efficiently. This may involve setting aside a half day when all routine meetings involving consultants are held, perhaps in conjunction with local continuing professional development (CPD) meetings at a common venue, thus reducing time wasted in travelling. Here are some ideas for evaluating the usefulness of routine meetings:

- What is the purpose of the meeting (eg information sharing, consultation or decision-making)?
- What are the alternative methods of achieving this purpose (eg a monthly 'news' bulletin, consultation by email or by using a trained interviewer to elicit opinion)?
- Are any of them equally or more effective and/or more efficient?
- If it is a decision-making meeting, does it (or do the people attending it) have the authority to make the relevant decisions?
- Am I the right person to attend?
- When will the meeting start and when will it finish? (see Box 6.1)

When possible, more efficient and effective communication and decision-making methods should be used. If there is a genuine need for a meeting, then clearly it should be conducted efficiently and effectively. It is essential that a meeting has an end time as well a beginning and that this is adhered to unless there are truly exceptional circumstances. For a more formal meeting, it is then the job of the chair to set and circulate in advance an agenda that can be effectively dealt with in the time available. All participants should come to the meeting properly prepared, and the chair needs to ensure that an appropriate time is devoted to each item on the agenda. Whenever possible, supporting papers should be circulated in advance. If papers have to be tabled because of urgency, they should be brief (no more than one side of A4). Teleconferencing and online meetings provide alternatives to face-to-face meetings that have advantages and disadvantages. The use of laptops or monitors rather than paper copies of documents saves paper but may reinforce the tendency to overload meetings with more information than can usefully be processed. Where technology is used it needs to be foolproof and efficient. Wasting time waiting for a teleconferencing connection or a file that won't load on screen is nobody's idea of fun.

BOX 6.1: Quote from a doctor with management, clinical and academic responsibility

'One of the big irritations for me is attending meetings with no clear finishing time or meetings that finish late, meaning I have to leave early and miss conclusions or arrive late for the next meeting or clinical task'.

Different types of meetings

We need to distinguish between different kinds of meetings:

- Highly structured business meetings that have a clearly defined managerial task such as
  - Board meetings (especially the Annual General Meeting)
  - Other routine meetings for operational, consultative and communication purposes
  - Project meetings with a clearly defined task or issue, usually time-limited
- Less structured meetings intended to
  - Improve communication and understanding between staff
  - Develop ideas for innovation
  - Support team and individual development

HIGHLY STRUCTURED MEETINGS

The Annual General Meeting and Board Meetings have legal significance and follow a carefully laid-out structure with agenda and papers circulated in advance. Other routine meetings such as *Drugs and Therapeutics Committees* also require clear terms of reference and a relatively formal approach.

Often the chairing of routine meetings can be used as an opportunity to develop the skills of doctors in this area. It does not all need to be done by doctors with substantial management roles. Whoever chairs the meeting, it is vital that all those attending are properly prepared and make constructive contributions that move things forward. Developing a culture that is task-focused in this type of meeting is important.

In addition to routine meetings, there are also meetings with a fixed lifespan to do with managing specific issues or projects. Again, it is important that such meetings are kept to task and that necessary work is done between meetings to carry the work forward. Otherwise the meeting can become a substitute for real work and action and can delay rather than advance the project it is overseeing. It is also important that such meetings have a clear purpose, appropriate authority and a life that ends when the task is completed (or when it becomes obvious that the task never will be completed). Redundant meetings waste everybody's time. The cost of meetings with senior staff is very significant not only in terms of wasted time (and money) but also in terms of making days more stressful for those whose days are often already more than full. This is a point to re-iterate how important it is for meetings to finish on time so that people can get on with the other things that are important in their work life, especially for those with clinical commitments.

For smaller task-oriented meetings, it increases efficiency if the minutes are kept as action notes and agreed *at the meeting when decisions are made* rather than written up and presented at the next meeting. Action notes should be just that. They should record the agreed decision, the action that flows from it, who has responsibility for the action and a timescale for carrying it through. At the next meeting, people should be held to account and asked to report progress (or completion) on the actions agreed at the previous meeting. There is nothing more exasperating than going to an action-orientated meeting and finding that nothing has moved forward since the last one. If that happens, one should seriously and openly question the usefulness of the meeting.

When chairing meetings, it is vital that you set a good example in defining the purpose (and, when appropriate, the authority) of the meeting. You should then structure the meeting to ensure it delivers on its purpose. The Whitmore GROW model (Goals, Reality, Options, Will for action) [1] has already been mentioned as a useful way of structuring decision-making (Box 4.2). It entails first being clear about the purpose of the meeting and its Goals. For more formal meetings, the agenda will need to be set out in some detail in advance; but for less formal, smaller meetings, the detailed agenda can be modified and agreed at the beginning. This can then become the agreed agenda and for each item a purpose should be agreed. The next step is to be explicit, for each item, about making sure that all aspects of the Reality of the situation are 'on the table'. Then it moves to exploring all the Options for achieving the goals for each item before finally settling on a Will for action (who does what and when by). This, combined with minutes in the form of action notes and a chair who holds people to account for agreed action, can do a lot to improve the efficiency and effectiveness of meetings (including clinical decision-making meetings).

LESS STRUCTURED MEETINGS

These meetings are usually facilitated rather than chaired. Facilitation of meetings is a learned skill that involves developing

- An understanding of what participants want
- An agreed agenda and process
- An understanding of the reality of the issues and the perspectives of the participants
- Creative options and decisions on the way forward (where appropriate)

Facilitating meetings is a genuine opportunity to open up discussions and break entrenched positions, if you can manage the discussion. The experience of adult education is that how you start meetings is key and by opening up discussions by genuinely asking people what issues need to be covered and shaping the agenda, you will find that important issues emerge, often for the first time. Following is a technique that you can use for this type of meeting in both short and extended versions.

EXERCISE 6.1
Listening swap

This is an activity developed by www.survivingwork.org that you can use at the beginning of any meeting or group discussion, based on adult education methods. You can do it as a simple exercise in listening or as the start of a larger group discussion about issues at work. This activity works very well in healthcare settings as it is an efficient way of getting to the bottom of problems when people feel they don't have time. It also ensures that you start off meetings with people actually listening to each other. Although we know the theory, listening is something that is very rarely practiced in systems under stress.

To open up a meeting, ask people to talk about what the issues are for them at work. You can phrase this in an open way. What brought you here today? What are the issues that really need to be covered in this meeting? If your meeting has been called to cover a particular theme such as team communications, you could ask 'Why are people not speaking up at work?' The less prescriptive the better, as people are being asked to really say what is on their mind, rather than yours.

Ask participants to work in pairs, each person will spend 5 minutes just listening to their partner. Listeners should be asked to remain attentive, to listen but not to interrupt or ask questions of the speaker even if there are silences. At the end of 5 minutes, the partners are asked to swap round where the listener is now speaking.

At the end you can ask people to raise the issues that came out of the listening swap which then form the agenda for the rest of the meeting. If you are working in a large group, you can ask people to work in small groups of 6–10 people to discuss the key themes that have come up.

What is important in this activity is that you encourage people to practice really listening for 5 minutes – a revelation to most people is how much information can be conveyed if you just listen. Also, that you use the issues that people have raised to focus your discussions in the remainder of the meeting. If you're going to ask people what they think, you have to show that it matters what they say.

Reviewing the meetings you attend

From time to time it is useful to review the meetings you attend and think through whether there are any meetings that are unnecessary or, equally important, whether there are any meetings that you should be attending or developing (see Exercise 6.2).

EXERCISE 6.2
Reviewing the meetings you attend

Look through your diary for the last month and list the meetings you were expected to attend. For the more formal meetings listed, make a note of the purpose and whether the meeting achieved its purpose. If you are in a position to do so, question whether there are more efficient and effective ways of achieving the objectives of these meetings (using the ideas listed earlier in this chapter). You could also consider scrapping meetings whose purpose can be better served in other ways. Consider not attending meetings where your presence makes no difference (or perhaps pairing with a trusted colleague so that each of you attends every other meeting). Rigorously examine how each meeting is conducted and whether you could make it more effective and efficient. (This is generally easiest if you chair the meeting; but sometimes possible if you enjoy a good relationship with the chair and can influence them to alter the conduct of the meeting.) Expect this exercise to liberate some time that you can use for other purposes, including less structured, more developmental meetings of the kind discussed earlier.

RAISING CONCERNS AND DUTY OF CARE

In this section, we will first consider the issues around raising concerns and the duty of care that devolves on all staff in the National Health Service (NHS). We will then go on to consider the special considerations that apply to doctors with management responsibilities.

For all NHS staff

In the current NHS context, one of the difficult areas for staff is whether to raise concerns over a lack of resources, a concern for the vast majority of clinicians. The professional advice is that if you know that there is a serious problem with lack of resources, then you are obliged to raise your concerns.

The NHS Constitution sets the principles for how healthcare is delivered. It was amended in 2015 to respond to the Francis inquiries and includes a requirement for

- Patient involvement
- Providing feedback
- Duty of candour
- Raising complaints
- Respecting staff rights, responsibilities and commitments
- Embodying dignity, respect and compassion

For health and social care professionals, this raises the potential for refusing instructions where it threatens to breach your duty of care, part of your professional code. In this situation, the professional has a personal duty of care to provide good clinical care and with it a Duty of Candour (enacted in 2014) to raise concerns about poor practice with patients and employers.

Many NHS organisations have standardised ways of reporting incidents and concerns. The Virginia Mason Production System (VMPS) discussed in Chapter 8 tries to emulate the quality control methods of the Toyota Production system by making it very easy for any member of staff to trigger a patient safety alert [2].

Concerns about risk to patient safety may arise from

- *Human error*: Inadvertent action and mistakes
- *At-risk behaviour*: Actions that are consciously taken that increase risk, which are either not recognised or are believed to be acceptable
- *Reckless behaviour*: Where unjustifiable and substantial risk is consciously taken

Many healthcare organisations will require any events (or behaviour) involving the safety or well-being of a patient (including 'near misses') to be reported as an incident or alert. Often these will be colour coded, with the most serious incidents coded red. It is important to be aware of the reporting system in your own organisation. Concerns about treatment of staff (eg bullying) or issues of staff fitness for work also need to be addressed and organisations should have clear pathways for dealing with these.

Whether or not an issue needs to be processed through the reporting system or whether it can be dealt with informally will depend on the severity of the problem, the degree of risk involved and whether the situation responds to attempts at informal resolution. If you are, for example, concerned that a colleague is overstressed it may be appropriate to first discuss the issue with them. If you are concerned about a workplace issue, it is worth sounding out colleagues informally about whether they also have concerns. If so, some form of joint action may be more effective than an individual one whether in offering informal support or in reporting the concern more formally.

If you have concerns as an individual, before you start:

- Be clear about your concerns and their level of urgency.
- Set out the issues clearly for yourself.
- Decide, preferably with the support of colleagues, whether the issue can be handled informally or whether the concern needs to be raised with managers through the formal reporting system.
- Be clear about the outcomes you are seeking.
- Make sure you are aware of the systems and policies in your organisation.

If informal contact does not work, you will need to raise your concerns at an appropriate level of management. This should be done carefully to avoid 'blame' and including organisational or contextual factors that may be influencing the practice. You may also want to speak to the British Medical Association (BMA) or other union representative (including representatives of defence unions where appropriate) – particularly if the issues relate to health and safety concerns, workloads or staff shortages.

The most consistent piece of advice is to try to raise concerns informally either directly with the people concerned or with your direct manager, or both. Formal channels should only be used when other options have been exhausted, except where there is immediate risk that cannot be managed in any other way.

For doctors with management responsibilities

Managers have a responsibility to manage concerns – including having informal meetings and cross-checking concerns against policies and standards. Managers are expected to use a wide range of skills in these processes including confidentiality, maintaining channels of communication, following formal procedures.

Managers and NHS Board members' responsibilities include

- Putting in place systems and policies that allow for concerns to be raised and investigated
- Ensuring that staff are not restricted or afraid of raising concerns
- Ensuring that staff understand their duty of candour
- Ensuring that people that raise concerns are not victimised or penalised

Box 6.2 contains a useful checklist for anyone considering raising a concern.

BOX 6.2: Raising concerns checklist

- Are you clear what you are concerned about and why? What evidence do you have and, if appropriate, can you get more?
- Does this issue affect you, or can you raise your concerns collectively? If no one else wants to raise your concerns, you should still raise them.
- Have you placed your concerns 'on the record'? Even if you raised them verbally, it is essential that there is an audit trail. Such evidence is essential to protect patients (and yourself).
- Have you set out what you want to achieve? Before you raise your concern, be as clear as you can what you want to achieve.
- Is it possible to work together with your employer to address your concerns? It may not be, but if it is, respond positively.
- Check your employer's procedures for raising and escalating concerns.
- Set out in a single statement what your concerns are, the evidence in support, what you want done, when and why.
- If you are offered a meeting, do not just turn up for the meeting, prepare for it. Make sure there is a professional, accountable, relationship between those raising concerns and anyone accompanying or representing you such as a trade union rep.

MANAGING CONFLICT

Conflict will always occur but opportunities for unnecessary conflict can and should be minimised. That is not to say that disagreement should be avoided or dissenting opinions suppressed. An organisation with a clear sense of its purpose and values will be less likely to generate internal and external conflict than one that lacks such clarity. To reduce the likelihood of conflict an organisation and its management needs to adhere to the following principles and behaviours:

- Different opinions are sought and valued from all relevant parties.
- Time is taken to consult and obtain consensus.
- The need to deliver care and treatment in a timely way is recognised.
- Standards are agreed with practitioners and service users and carers as well as commissioners.

When conflict does occur, it should be dealt with quickly and effectively before it has time to develop a self-perpetuating momentum. Where conflict is over a genuine difference of opinion or priorities, the principles of *negotiation* (see Chapter 5) are most useful. We need to separate the people from the problem and focus on interests not positions. We need to work with the parties to the conflict to look for solutions that are an improvement on the *status quo* for all parties. Finally, in choosing between them, we need to devise objective criteria that are acceptable to all. This is no small task, and arbitration and conciliation are full-time tasks for some people. One of the most difficult things in life is dealing with conflict. Some ideas for handling conflict are summarised in Box 6.3.

BOX 6.3: Containing conflict

- Don't ignore the danger signs and put off addressing the problem.
- Try to pre-empt conflict by setting a time to talk to the people involved, preferably somewhere quiet and not at the end of a long day.
- Set a time limit for the conversation and establish that the focus is to find a solution.
- Acknowledge the problem at work and the realities that need to be dealt with.
- Try to avoid too much joking or being clever – much better to be clear to avoid confusion.
- Listen to the other person and try not to interrupt.
- If there is no obvious solution, try to agree at least one next step.
- Make sure that you agree your next contact with each other.

We hope that you are not currently involved in any conflicts. Exercise 6.3 is designed to help you develop your skills in this area.

> **EXERCISE 6.3**
> **Managing conflict**
>
> Consider an area in which there has been recent (possibly unnecessary) conflict in your area of work. How could it have been prevented? How could lessons learned from this conflict help prevent future problems? Has the conflict been resolved? If so, how? If not, what would it take to resolve the conflict? If you have a current conflict to resolve, apply the previous ideas and use negotiating skills to see if you can resolve it more effectively.

If you are a manager involved in resolving conflict, it is important not to get 'hooked' into supporting one side over the other. That is not to say that your assessment of the situation is unimportant. You may make a rational decision to support one side, but this should not be on the basis of whom you like or find most appealing. A particular feature of some conflicts was described many years ago by Karpman [3], a transactional analyst who described the 'drama' triangle (also known as the 'victim triangle'), in which people act out their emotional needs in a non-constructive way. The three roles in this triangle are labelled 'victim', 'persecutor' and 'rescuer'. Just as those described as bullies are often the victim of bullying, so those who play the role of persecutor may perceive themselves as victims. Indeed, the roles are interchangeable.

CASE STUDY 6.1: VICTIM TRIANGLE

A junior doctor complains to the College Tutor that the consultant she works for is treating her unfairly. The junior doctor alleges that the consultant is asking her to see too many 'new' patients and has unrealistic expectations of how quickly she can dictate clinic and discharge letters. She is 'at the end of her tether' and tearfully says she is on the point of resigning from the rotation. Because of the perceived urgency of the situation, the College Tutor (with the agreement of the junior doctor) phones the consultant and asks what is going on. The consultant says she was unaware of any problems. She had been asking the junior to see the same number of new patients each week as the previous junior and had only been trying to maintain the standards demanded by the Trust in terms of timeliness of letters. Indeed, the service manager had been putting pressure on her because letters from her team were in danger of breaching Trust standards in terms of promptness. She feels she is being put under unreasonable pressure by the tutor and reminds her that her specialty doctor has been off sick for 6 months, leading to increased pressure on herself. She feels people are making unreasonable demands and threatens to 'take out a grievance'. At this point, the tutor, remembering the 'victim triangle', realises

(Continued)

CASE STUDY 6.1: (Continued) VICTIM TRIANGLE
that she has started off by playing rescuer and is now in danger of becoming 'persecutor', whilst the consultant, perceived as persecutor by the junior doctor, is in danger of becoming 'victim'. She realises this is a maladaptive dynamic and seeks a more effective way of dealing with the situation.

We have probably all come upon such examples in our daily lives in the highly pressurised atmosphere of providing healthcare. You may want to take a few moments to think of how, in the example earlier, the clinical tutor could take things forward in a constructive way.

STRATEGIC THINKING

This is a vital function in any organisation (and clearly related to change management and leadership, discussed in more detail in Chapter 8). The decision-making framework in Figure 4.1 can also be used for strategic planning. A healthcare provider organisation needs to think about its 'customers' and what they are likely to want to purchase over the next planning period (realistically no more than 3–5 years in the current NHS). The term 'customer' does not sit easily with traditional healthcare practice in the UK. It refers to the patients (service users) but more directly to the people who purchase the services the organisation provides. For General practitioners (GPs), as discussed earlier, this is effectively the patient who elects to use their services. For secondary care organisations for the last 5 years it has been Care Commissioning Groups (CCGs) purchasing on behalf of patients, though individual treatment and referral decisions may be taken by service users in partnership with their own GPs. The Accountable Care Organisations/Systems/Partnerships (ACOs) that are emerging from the Sustainability and Transformation Plans make the future less certain. Although the direction of travel is in favour of increased privatisation of services, the future is again deeply uncertain.

Devising a strategy in the light of such uncertainty is not easy. However, the attempt has to be made. A strategy needs many component parts, some of which are listed in Box 6.4. These are essentially the elements of strategy for an organisation operating in a market place. The NHS in England, at secondary care level, has effectively been turned into a fragmented market place, with provider Trusts and other organisations having to plan according to market principles. The whole thing is held together by the function of CCGs and NHS England commissioning services appropriately. The *Five Year Forward View* and subsequent Sustainability and Transformation Plans (STPs) appear to be an attempt to reintroduce more integrated strategic planning. As we go to press, it remains to be seen how these and the ACS will develop and whether they will further the agenda of increasing privatisation or whether the NHS in England will once again return to being publicly provided as well as funded. Scotland and Wales have followed their own paths with more centralised public planning and provision.

BOX 6.4: Some component parts of a strategy for a healthcare organisation

- *Overall strategy*: Concerned with the purpose and values of the organisation and where it wants to be in terms of that purpose in (say) 3 years' time. This is really a time-limited expression of the purpose, vision and values of a 'mission' statement.
- *Product development strategy*: How it will develop the range of products needed to maintain or improve its position as a provider.
- *Marketing strategy*: How it will make sure that purchasers and users of services are well informed about the range and quality of services it provides and the benefits it offers over competitors and how it will keep itself informed about what the purchaser wants and is likely to want in the future.
- *Staffing strategy*: How it will attract and keep the staff it needs to deliver its core services.
- *Quality and effectiveness strategy*: How it will set and maintain quality and standards of provision and measure health outcomes.
- *Financial strategy*: How it will make sure that the financial resources it attracts are sufficient to cover its costs (and make a return for shareholders if it is a commercial organisation).
- *Risk-management strategy*: How it will manage all kinds of risk, including financial and clinical risk. This may include divesting itself of functions (including some support services) that can be bought in under contractual arrangements that spread risk.

These components are not necessarily all that need to be considered. and they can be 'chunked' in different ways (eg financial risk may be considered principally as part of the financial strategy and clinical risk as part of the quality and effectiveness agenda). Some organisations will have a separate 'communications' strategy, others will consider this part of 'marketing'.

OVERALL STRATEGY

This is really a time-limited expression of the consequences of the purpose, vision and values of a 'mission' statement, which is the foundation on which the whole strategy rests. It includes a realistic assessment of where the organisation is, where it wants to be, what resources it is likely to need to get there and what obstacles stand in the way (including competition from commercial providers). In other 'market-places' there is a recognised pattern of so-called 'big money' running services at a loss, sometimes over many years in order to undercut other providers in order to achieve market domination at which point they can raise prices and generate huge long-term profits. It is to be hoped this will not be the fate of the NHS in England. An estimate that the financial climate is hostile may cause an organisation to 'trim its sails' and have a less ambitious 3-year plan, or it may cause it to look for areas where it can bring 'in-house' services that are currently being purchased from other

Table 6.1 STEP and SWOT analysis

Social	Strengths
Technological	Weaknesses
Economic	Opportunities
Political	Threats

providers at a premium. In mental health, for example, there may be the issue of bringing some secure services currently purchased from a commercial provider into the locality and providing better services at lower cost as part of an overall 'deal' with purchasers. Once all this is carefully assessed, the various component parts of the strategy need to be developed. Two 'tools' mentioned in Chapter 3 are commonly used in constructing a strategy (Table 6.1). One, 'STEP' (Social, Technical, Economic, Political) (or 'PEST') analysis, looks primarily at the external business environment and has been discussed earlier in this chapter in the context of change management; the other, 'SWOT' (Strengths, Weaknessed, Opportunities, Threats) analysis, looks at the organisation itself, its strengths and weaknesses, and the opportunities and threats that the (ever-changing) environment offers and poses.

We considered some of the *social* trends in the UK and European cultures more generally in Chapter 3. In the last 50 years or so, we have moved from a 'post-war consensus' about public services and the nature of society to a more strongly capitalist and consumerist position. Centralised planning has become unpopular. Paradoxically, *over-regulation* of public services has become endemic, despite the fact that we are suffering from an *economic* downturn as a result of the 'greed' of *under-regulated* capitalism in areas like banking. The *political* dominance of the capitalist market model has been growing even though its weaknesses have long been known even to its proponents [4]. It is now coming under public scrutiny and a more egalitarian co-operative model may ensue. This is the political economic and social context within which we have to plan. *Technology* is also important in all areas of medicine. This may be high-cost equipment and its use (Magnetic Resonance Imaging [MRI] scanners, for example) or expensive new drugs, but it may also be the technology of delivering (for example) talking therapy of a good standard to all who need it.

Wishful thinking has no place in strategic planning. The authors would be more comfortable in a world where the greed and wastefulness of the world's resources that characterise the worst forms of neo-liberal capitalism were less dominant and where the very rich were not quite so rich and the very poor not quite so poor. Really, this desire for a fairer, more equal society is not just 'wishful thinking'. There is a sound evidence base establishing that more equal societies are healthier in many respects [5,6]. These ideas can be part of the value system of how an organisation strives to achieve its mission, but no organisation that wants to thrive in a market economy can ignore present reality.

Predicting the future of technology is also notoriously difficult. Not only the technology but also attitudes towards its use are changing all the time. This is one reason for adopting the relatively short time horizon of 3–5 years. Isolation hospitals for smallpox, TB sanatoria and, to a large extent, the old mental hospitals have all disappeared as a result primarily of technological change though, social, economic and political factors have played a part.

In dementia care, if someone were to invent a drug that halted the progress of Alzheimer's dementia, the whole focus of services would need to shift to the early detection of Alzheimer's disease or, better, the detection of those at risk of developing the disease, so that treatment could be instituted before there was significant brain damage. Such a treatment would also probably reduce lengths of stay in hospital for other conditions quite dramatically, reduce the incidence of delirium and, in the longer term, reduce dramatically the need for residential care. Similarly, a medical cure for bowel cancer would dramatically reduce the need for colorectal surgery. These are the kind of things we need to think about.

EXERCISE 6.4
STEP analysis

If you are in a health provider organisation, spend half an hour thinking through how STEP analysis informs your ideas of what the service will be like in 3 years' time. If you are a GP, you may want to think through how you will be affected by the evolution of new healthcare systems that may integrate primary care and secondary care (eg see the Primary Care Home projects discussed briefly in Chapter 8). If you work in a different healthcare system, adapt the exercise to the needs of your organisation. Consider how much flexibility you need to retain to deal with unanticipated developments.

The next stage is to look at the strengths and weaknesses of your current organisation. Often, when people do this, they find that some of the weaknesses 'flow' from some of the strengths and vice versa. Try to be realistic and 'hard-nosed' about strengths and weaknesses. If you think your organisation is a pleasant place to work, what is the evidence for that in terms of recruitment, retention, contentment and reduced sick leave in members of staff. In other words, try to find objective data to support your ideas.

EXERCISE 6.5
SWOT analysis

DO IT! In two columns list the strengths and weaknesses of your organisation (or your part of it). Consider whether and how they make it fit to survive and thrive in its current (ever-changing) environment. Specifically, look at the strengths first and ask how these can be marketed, developed, generalised and otherwise exploited. Many people make the mistake of concentrating only on weaknesses, but often concentrating on building strengths can be more productive. Now look at the areas of weakness. If it were up to you, would you want to rectify these areas and, if so, how would you set about the task? The alternative, if the weakness is in an area that is not part of the core business of the organisation, is to think about whether services could be bought in from another provider or perhaps strengthened by forming a collaboration or consortium with other organisations.

Now you should be in a position to clearly identify the opportunities and threats that the next 3 years offer to your organisation. How will you seize these opportunities and neutralise the threats? Always bear in mind the need to maintain direction and flexibility even in the face of the relentless change imposed by politicians, technology and social developments.

So that is it – an overview of strategic planning in a nutshell; though, of course, strategic planning for the organisation is usually done on a collective basis and implementation requires the skills and attributes described in Chapter 8 on innovation and entrepreneurship.

PRODUCT DEVELOPMENT STRATEGY

This goes hand in hand with marketing strategy; there is no point in developing products (services) that nobody who is in a position to purchase them wants to buy. At the same time, doctors driven by the imperative to provide the best healthcare possible (within available resources) to their population may have strong ideas about services they want to develop. It is very important that the voices of senior clinicians are sufficiently heard in the process of developing services. It is part of the Medical Director's job to make sure that all senior clinicians (especially doctors) are heard as services are continually redesigned. It is also part of the medical manager's job to offer sound advice to the organisation about priorities, feasibility and *training needs* if new models of service are to be initiated.

CASE STUDY 6.2: NEW WAYS OF WORKING

A mental health trust decides to institute a functional separation between inpatient and community care. To some extent, this is politically driven by the mandate to introduce 'New Ways of Working'. Nevertheless, for the general psychiatric services it makes sense because the shrinking bed-base means that there are too many consultant teams working on each ward. By making one or two consultants responsible for inpatients, the number of ward rounds is reduced and other consultants spend all or most of their clinical time in the community, where most modern psychiatric care is located, with their teams. The medical manager's job is to anticipate problems (eg who has authority to admit and discharge, how continuity of care between hospital and community will be achieved). The medical manager may also need to prevent overenthusiasm for change for change's sake! Do the services for elderly people require the same functional separation? Or does it make more sense with the lower number of consultants, the relatively higher frequency of hospitalisation and the overriding need for continuity of care to maintain the 'old-fashioned' model of *integrated care* with the same team providing inpatient and community care? The final answer will differ depending on factors like the

---

(Continued)

> ### CASE STUDY 6.2: (Continued) NEW WAYS OF WORKING
>
> size of the area covered, the geographical characteristics of the area, the location of inpatient beds and other issues. The point is that somebody needs to ask the question. That somebody is usually a senior clinician or a medical manager; if it is a senior clinician, the medical manager should take the point seriously and seek to develop a consensus with other senior clinicians about the best way forwards. As far as possible, any consensus should be evidence based. Another aspect of 'New Ways of Working' is that more initial assessments are done in the community by non-medical members of the team. Managers who are not clinicians do not always realise that other disciplines need training and preferably standardised methods of assessment if they are to make appropriate assessments and recognise those who need urgent action (including referral for urgent psychiatric/medical opinion).

We have drawn this example from mental health services because this is the area with which we are most familiar. At the moment, these services are under financial and recruitment pressures, resulting from politically driven 'austerity'. Following the development of crisis teams, assertive outreach teams, early onset psychosis teams and other as well as community mental health teams, the dangers of fragmentation are becoming more apparent. What will happen next remains to be seen.

We are sure that you will be familiar in your area with other elements of service re-design where only a senior clinician (usually a doctor-manager) can anticipate some of the problems likely to arise and try to ensure these issues are dealt with in advance.

MARKETING STRATEGY

A marketing strategy is about many things:

- Consumer/purchaser awareness
- Horizon scanning
- Communication
- Image and 'brand' awareness
- Advertising products

As the health service in the UK, and especially in England, becomes more fragmented and commercialised, these issues may be of increasing importance. On the other hand, the tide may be turning about the privatisation of public services.

Consumer/purchaser awareness needs to be developed. In the UK for the GP, the consumer (ie patients on the practice list or coming through the door in open access services) is essentially equivalent to the purchaser (in reality in England, it is NHS England who actually commission primary care services). For the doctor in a secondary care trust, the purchaser is likely to be a CCG, choosing on behalf of (or with) the patient. How purchaser-provider decisions will be made under STPs has yet to be established. Presumably this will involve groups of CCGs acting together to purchase services in a single geographical area (or 'footprint'). The provider needs to be aware of what the consumer *wants*. (If, however, the purpose of the organisation is to provide high-quality healthcare, not turn a profit, the provider must also take into account what the consumer *needs*, which is not always the same thing.) One way of squaring the circle is to ensure that consumers are well educated so that they understand the difference between wants and needs and know what they need as well as what they want. In a service that strives to provide equitable access there are further problems in that some groups of consumers can be more vocal than others and providing a luxury service for the vocal might mean providing no service at all for relatively undemanding groups like old people. In privately funded services (like those in the USA until very recently), there has been the paradox of incredibly good (even excessive) services for rich people and nothing at all for poor people. Nevertheless, the principle remains that it is important to have a two-way dialogue with one's patients/customers/consumers/ service users/clients. The emergence of ACOs, including experiments like the Primary Care Home teams discussed in Chapter 8, may lead to new considerations in this area.

CASE STUDY 6.3 TRANSFORMING SERVICES IN DORSET

This summary comes from the work of Phil Richardson, a doctor working with Dorset CCG to restructure primary care services. This summary offers his top 10 tips for transformation:

- *Information*: Healthcare workers are motivated by comparative data and charts.
- *Communication*: Remember that this is a two-way process.
- *Innovation*: Set up events and network meetings where people can genuinely exchange experience and best practice including inviting guest speakers.
- *Shared understanding*: This requires listening rather than broadcasting ideas. Take the time to genuinely listen to providers, service users and colleagues.

(Continued)

CASE STUDY 6.3: (Continued) TRANSFORMING SERVICES IN DORSET

- *Leadership*: Being clear about the focus of the transformation. Using working groups and delegated leadership so change is not reliant on one person.
- *Vision*: People stretch into visions they are really attracted to such as really enjoying work again.
- *Buy-in*: Answer the question 'what's in it for me?'
- *Readiness*: Make sure you know who is ready to move now and who isn't and plan accordingly.
- *Empowerment*: Don't ask permission, trust each other and take active responsibility for bringing good ideas.
- *Stakeholder engagement*: Find what we have in common that is a basis for us to work together.

The 10 points in case study 6.3 are reinforced by some of the principles about influencing people discussed in Chapter 5 and about change management discussed in Chapter 8.

Horizon scanning is a jargon way of saying 'being aware of what's on the way'. This is often particularly hard for clinicians with very busy services. It is hard to 'keep your eyes on the horizon' when 'your nose is to the grindstone'. Scanning the horizon needs to take into account socio-demographic projections (need for more services for older people and for children of immigrants for example), technological innovation, economic projections and the ever-changing manifestations of political ideology.

Communication about the organisation and the services it provides should be part of every marketing strategy. Although the first step is listening, it is also very important to be heard on fair and equitable terms. Organisations that provide healthcare need to communicate not only when things go well, but perhaps even more importantly, to communicate clearly, honestly and with a degree of humility when things go wrong.

'Image' or 'brand' awareness with the local public, purchasers and service users helps sell services in a market. The idea of working to maintain a public image does not appeal to many doctors and 'branding' is often used commercially to maximise profits from a gullible public. However, if the image offered corresponds to the truth about the organisation (ie if there is integrity in the branding), then it is a way of building public and patient confidence in the provider. Like it or not, public confidence is important.

The General Medical Council has generally taken a dim view of doctors *advertising* to the public and in the UK direct advertising of prescription-only medicines to the public has also been severely limited. However, if the movement into a more commercially oriented marketplace continues, providers will need to learn how to advertise and sell their products to purchasers. Part of the story is building good and trusting relationships with purchasers. Being honest, reliable, competitive, well informed and providing consistently high-quality services that meet the purchaser's needs is probably the best advert of all; but these qualities need somehow to be brought to the attention of the purchasers who might otherwise not realise what a good deal they are getting.

Of course, product development strategy and marketing strategy are very closely intertwined and some would see product development as part of marketing.

STAFFING STRATEGY

Nationally, there is a growing concern about the workforce crisis within specific professional groups including nurses, midwives, mental health workers and GPs. This reality is very hard for individuals to manage, but the reality is that workforce planning, even in a context of scarcity, still has to be done at the organisational level, requiring up-to-date information on national, regional and local staffing issues.

Broadly, there are three elements to any staffing strategy. One is predicting the competences and therefore the numbers of different types of staff that will be needed in the future. The next is working out how to ensure that sufficient people are trained in each discipline and, finally, working out how to attract and keep good staff members (which has to do with the culture of the organisation and the quality of its employment practices). Medical managers will most often be concerned with the medical component of a staffing strategy, but it will be led by human resources specialists (if the strategy is led at all). This will expose some tensions within systems, where the temptation will be to recruit non-clinical and more junior clinicians just to cut the wages bill.

QUALITY AND EFFECTIVENESS

These are very important indeed and every organisation needs to have a strategy and a culture that ensures that quality and effectiveness are centre stage. This is the subject of the next chapter, so we will not consider it further here.

FINANCIAL STRATEGY

Like staffing strategy, this is a specialist area best led by finance people. However, finance (like staffing) is a means to the end of providing good healthcare, and as such it should not dominate planning, but should provide financial boundaries within which service development, marketing, quality and effectiveness need to operate.

RISK-MANAGEMENT STRATEGY

Risk management has become a powerful force within business and public services over the last half century. It embraces all areas of function, from finance to floor polish. Doctors will be most familiar with clinical risk management where the risks of a particular course of treatment or operation are thought through in advance, minimised as far as possible and explained carefully to the patient. However, it also applies to decisions about how many nurses to employ and whether to use locums or agency staff. Doctor-managers will be most concerned about clinical risk management and risk management in areas of medical employment. Although it may be feasible to have a broad risk-management strategy that details the organisation's general approach to the avoidance, minimisation and management of risk. This is also likely to be a 'heading' that must be considered in other components of strategy.

BUSINESS PLANNING

If the strategic plan for an organisation has a (rolling) 3- or 5-year horizon, the business plan is much more focused, dealing with the current year. Provider organisations usually have an overarching corporate plan and then business plans for each business centre/unit or clinical directorate. Specific projects also need to have a business plan (this has a lot in common with a research protocol but does not go through such stringent ethical scrutiny). The corporate plan includes the plans of the individual business units/directorates, takes account of purchasers' intentions and is consistent with the overall strategic plan. It is generally produced over several iterations between purchasers, corporate provider and business units and is sometimes not completed by the time the relevant financial year starts.

Anthony Young [7] describes the business plan for a directorate as 'a simple exercise in common sense' which must be consistent with corporate objectives for the year'. He provides a series of helpful questions to consider in developing a business plan as follows:

- What is the period to be planned for?
- What do we want to do?
- What do others want us to do?
- What is the probable budget?
- How do we integrate these pressures?
- What resources will we need?
- What will be the effect on other directorates (business units)?

Although the *period to be planned for* is often next year, this is not always the case and there will usually be a strategic direction running over several years to be taken into account. This is necessary to ensure continuity since many developments take more than a year to realise. *What we want to do* consists of ideas from within the service, for example, developing a community service in place of a clinic or training up a group of staff to take on new responsibilities. *What others want us to do* are top-down demands from the organisation and 'sideways' demands from other business units as well as demands from service users and purchasers. The *probable budget* is hard to estimate and may get harder as purchasing arrangements are again revised. Usually (unless there are major new developments or planned retrenchments), the amount available last year is a good starting point with a notional uplift for inflation and some clawed back under the euphemistically termed 'efficiency savings'. *Integrating the pressures* from all these sources requires a lot of time and the involvement of as many people as possible within the business unit. There may be genuine savings that can be made, but people will often only be willing to bring forward ideas for savings if they can see how they and the unit they work for might benefit. *Resources needed* include staff, finance for recurrent and capital expenditure, services from other business units, and facilities. The *effect on other business units* and, sometimes, other organisations must also be considered, including costing any extra services needed.

Finally, somebody who writes well, who has been involved in the process and has some passion for it needs to sit down and write a draft. Such a draft can be structured into the following sections:

- Summary
- Introduction, including how the plan fits into the overall strategy of the unit and organisation and a brief STEP analysis (see earlier)
- Review of last year's plans and achievements
- Brief SWOT analysis (see earlier)
- The plan, including how current services will be maintained and how new developments will be progressed, with some details about who will lead and what resources will be needed and where they will come from
- How outcomes will be assessed
- An appendix of relevant data

FINANCIAL CONTROL

An organisation, business unit or clinical directorate has a budget to manage. This function is assisted by management accounting. The budget needs to be carefully set in the first place for the whole organisation and any business units individually. There will be clear rules about whether underspending on revenue can be spent on capital, who can authorise what kind of expenditure, whether and how money can be transferred between budgets and so on. The finance and accounting experts within the organisation will usually produce a forecast of total spend and spend under different headings ('lines') month by month and a monthly review of how spending is going. This gives an opportunity to adjust spending month on month to ensure that targets are met at the end of the year. It is important for medical managers to be involved in this process since they can often help the rest of the team understand why some areas are underspending and others overspending.

This is a very brief introduction to financial control, and this area may be of increasing importance in the UK if health services continue to be increasingly commercialised. A more detailed account (including a little about the intricacies of financial and cost accounting) can be found in Young's *The Medical Manager* [7]. Financial control will continue to be important whether the present trend towards increasing commercialisation of services continues or is reversed.

REFERENCES

1. Whitmore J (2017) *Coaching for Performance*. London, UK: Nicholas Brealey Publishing.
2. Kenney C (2010) *Transforming Health Care: Virginia Mason Medical Center's Pursuit of the Perfect Patient Experience* (p. 50). Boca Raton, FL: CRC Press.
3. Karpman S (1968) Fairy tales and script drama analysis. *Transactional Analysis Bulletin*, 7(26): 39–44.
4. Griffiths B (1989) *Morality and the Marketplace*, 2nd ed. London, UK: Hodder & Stoughton.
5. Wilkinson R and Pickett K (2010) *The Spirit Level: Why Equality Is Better for Everyone*. London, UK: Penguin Books.
6. Marmot M (2016) *The Health Gap: The Challenge of an Unequal World*. London, UK: Bloomsbury Paperbacks.
7. Young AE (2003) *The Medical Manager*. London, UK: BMJ Publishing Group.

7

Maintaining and improving quality

The quality challenge is perhaps the most significant the NHS has faced but we should approach it with confidence given what we have achieved to date.

David Nicholson
Former NHS Chief Executive (2010)

The concept of quality is not an easy one. The White Paper *Equity and Excellence: Liberating the NHS* distinguished three elements of quality: quality of health outcomes, safety and quality of the patient experience [1]. This has also more recently been emphasised by NHS England [2] in *The Five Year Forward View*. This has been an influential document and it has importantly highlighted the variability of 'quality' in different regions. It also emphasises the need to back local leadership and meaningful local flexibility to achieve the key objectives. From our point of view, safety can be subsumed under health outcomes and risk management since the quality of the patient experience is itself dependent on health outcomes and other dimensions:

- Health outcomes (related to evidence-based practice)
- Relationships
- Service experienced
- Management underpinning
- Timeliness
- Convenience
- Competent, compassionate, motivated staff
- Adequate numbers of staff, adequately supported

Of course, these dimensions are interrelated to some extent but it is possible, for example, to have a timely, convenient and friendly service that does not produce good health outcomes. If health outcomes are made the primary indicators of quality, then it is likely that to get them right, the other dimensions of quality will also need to be right. Sometimes some aspects of quality have to be reduced in order to provide quantity of service. Whilst this cannot be denied, it is also important to remember that sometimes improving quality can go hand in hand with improved productivity (see Case Study 7.1 and quality and productivity case studies on the Academy of Fabulous NHS Stuff – *www.fabnhsstuff.net*). The Virginia Mason Production System (VMPS) discussed in Chapter 8 also aims to improve both quality and productivity through staff engagement at all levels.

EVIDENCE-BASED PRACTICE AND HEALTH OUTCOMES

Good medical practice has always depended on learning from experience and thoughtful reflection. That is why doctors in training used to be encouraged to follow patients 'through the system' and see what became of them. But experience can sometimes be misleading. Why else would the fashion for 'bleeding' patients for all sorts of conditions have persisted so long in earlier times? Routine, valid, clinically relevant and reliable measures of outcomes should be used to ensure services are producing health improvement and to enable any changes in the system to be evaluated. This is quite a tall order! Outcomes are much easier to measure in some areas of medicine than others and persuading people to collect measures that they don't see as relevant is also an uphill and potentially futile struggle. Relating routine outcomes to a reliable and relevant evidence base remains a challenge.

In recent years evidence-based practice has come to rely increasingly on solid scientific methodologies. The most common of these is the systematic review of the evidence for the effectiveness of a particular treatment for a particular condition. For medication the well-conducted double-blind, randomised, placebo-controlled trial is the 'gold standard' and systematic reviews tend to value this kind of evidence most highly because it is less likely to be biased by human frailty and our tendency to see what we want to see. However, not everybody shares the medical scientist's preference for evidence which is, as far as humanly possible, free from bias and many other kinds of evidence will be brought forward to support particular points of view.

It is part of the role of the medical manager to stress the importance of well-conducted research as a basis for deciding where money should be spent. Not all of this will be double-blind, placebo-controlled, randomised evidence (see Case Study 7.1). However, whatever the methodology, it should be appropriate to the question asked and the research should be well conducted. Often, on the Board or within the directorate/business unit, the medical manager is the person best equipped to make judgements about the quality and relevance of research. Here is not the place to go into the details of evidence-based practice. Sackett and colleagues wrote what is still considered to be the authoritative work on the subject in 1996, *Evidence-based Medicine*, and now in its fourth edition [3]. Readers will be familiar with the method of asking the right question, critically examining the evidence and drawing valid conclusions. They will also know that, in most cases, evidence is examined systematically by organisations like the National Institute for Health and Clinical Excellence (NICE) to produce guidance that is helpful both to managers in making decisions about what services to provide or purchase and to clinicians in their daily work.

EXERCISE 7.1
Outcomes and evidence-based practice

Look at the area where you have management responsibility. How well (if at all) are the outcomes of interventions measured routinely? How far is the treatment provided evidence-based in terms of NICE or other recognised guidance or in terms of locally agreed evidence-based guidelines? Is there any area in which guidance needs to be implemented? What kind of change in outcomes would you expect? How can they be measured? If necessary, you may wish to perform or commission a formal clinical audit to answer some of these questions.

RELATIONSHIPS AND QUALITY

However good the medicine, if the doctor is rude, overbearing, curt and/or uncommunicative, the service user is unlikely to be satisfied. Worse, doctors with poor communication skills may fail to discover what is really bothering the patient and to gather the evidence needed for a sound diagnosis. On top of that, even if the right management is recommended, the service user may fail to follow the recommendations because of lack of trust in the doctor.

The quality of relationships tends to run through a team or organisation. We have probably all been to supermarkets or restaurants where members of staff are obviously disgruntled, often as a result of poor relationships with management. Health services are no different. Staff who are not given due respect and who are treated badly find it hard to treat patients well. There is a lot more about relationships in Chapter 2. They are foundational to a quality service.

SERVICE QUALITY

The quality of a service is essentially a function of the quality of its outcomes, how well it is organised and the quality of relationships within the organisation. How services are organised and the impact this has on the quality of the patient experience is amenable to research. Methods such as VMPS engage clinical staff and patients in service redesign to improve the quality of the experience (and often productivity too). At a more basic level, consumer research asks people what they think about different aspects of the service. Even when patients cannot give a good account of their experience (eg people with dementia) methods exist to enable quality to be assessed from the user's point of view (see Case Study 7.1).

CASE STUDY 7.1: DEMENTIA CARE MAPPING AND HOSPITAL TRANSPORT

The authors were party to a piece of work that used dementia care mapping to try to understand what made for high-quality ambulance transport for older people with dementia attending routine NHS clinic appointments. The end result was an improved service with escorts, improved understanding of the needs of people with dementia, more attention to their comfort and the avoidance of over long journey times. The new service was also less expensive. This study could never have been conducted using the double-blind, randomised, placebo-controlled trial methodology, but the mixed methodology applied was appropriate to the situation and produced worthwhile improvements in quality for patients [4].

MANAGEMENT QUALITY

The quality of management underpins the quality of the services that an organisation provides. Some of the important aspects of management quality that need to be maintained are as follows:

- Creating a culture of mutual respect where good relationships thrive
- Managing finances well so that money is always available to support clinical services
- Managing people well so that the right people are recruited and retained, absenteeism is minimised and the use of locum and agency staff restricted
- Corporate and clinical governance

The issues of relationships and organisational culture have been explored in some detail in Chapters 2 and 3. Financial management has been discussed briefly in Chapter 6. Managing people well follows from the culture of mutual respect but also requires good administration. Complex issues like on-call rotas, desynchronisation of annual leave for important staff groups, managing sickness absence, managing study leave and so on, call for good administration and procedures which are carried through swiftly and without fear or favour by medical managers and those who assist them. There is also the issue of giving people space to develop their competences and their own special interests (provided they can be dovetailed with the needs of the organisation and, ultimately, of patients). This will tend to lead to a more satisfied workforce. The example of NAViGO (a social enterprise) care in Chapter 8 demonstrates how several of these issues can be addressed.

Corporate governance is all about the integrity of the organisation and includes areas such as financial control and managers declaring any interests they may have when decisions are being made. Clinical governance is about creating an environment in which clinical excellence can flourish and includes elements of evidence-based practice, risk reduction and management as well as clinical audit and feedback (see the following).

EXERCISE 7.2
Measuring quality – some suggestions

List the ways in which your organisation, or the part of it for which you have responsibility, measures management quality. Regular anonymous surveys of staff help discover how well organisations are doing in maintaining a positive culture. Some organisations have policies for managing sick leave and helping people back to work as soon as possible. The impact of these can be measured by looking at sickness records. Do staff members take adequate amounts of appropriate study leave? Again, this can be monitored. Do doctors participate in local continuing professional development (CPD) activities? Is CPD properly supported and monitored to ensure that standards are met? These issues should be addressed by medical appraisal and revalidation systems. What is the rate of use of locums and agency staff? Is it regularly monitored? Is it satisfactory? What measures can be taken to improve recruitment and retention of permanent staff and how can this be monitored?

TIMELINESS AND CONVENIENCE

When people have a potentially life-threatening illness, timeliness becomes of utmost importance. The right treatment too late is useless. An appointment with a psychiatrist in 2 weeks or even 2 days is no use if the patient is severely depressed and acutely suicidal. Likewise, patients with suspected cancer should generally see the appropriate specialist as soon as possible and, in any case, within a week. For some other conditions, convenience will be more important than timeliness. For older people with limited mobility, services provided in the home or as close to it as possible are often more convenient. These things matter to patients and should always be considered when designing services.

EVIDENCE-BASED POLICY

Health policy tends to be based on a different kind of evidence to that which informs the practice of medicine. Comparative studies may show which ways of providing health services are most effective and efficient. Economic and political theories will also often be important in determining the policy framework for publicly funded services. The relatively recent *Five Year Forward View* is comprehensive and packed with ambition but has little good-quality evidence to support the proposed changes.

An area where there is a good basis for evidence-based policy is in the relationship between a more equal society and many measures of health and social well-being [5]. The research summarised in this work shows that, in richer countries, whether lesser degrees of income inequality between the top 20% income and the bottom 20% are achieved by more modest pay at the top or by progressive taxation, health and social outcomes tend to be better. This flies directly in the face of the unbridled capitalism that is politically so strong at present!

One of the jobs of the medical manager is to critically examine policy and ensure that it is not implemented in a naive way. Let us look at two examples from the proposals in *Equity and Excellence: Liberating the NHS* [1].

CASE STUDY 7.2: A NEEDS-LED APPROACH

One of the underpinning values of the *Equity and Excellence* was stated to be fairness, including a 'ban on age discrimination'. Previous anti-ageism campaigns had led some managers to try to abolish specialist old age mental health services on the ground that such specialist services were 'ageist'. In fact, the reason for the existence of specialist services was that older people with mental health problems have special needs that are best met by specialist services, and there is an international evidence base to support this. Despite this, when the principles of *Equity and Excellence* were implemented through the Health and Social Care Act (2012), campaigns had to be fought to stop managers in some areas simply abolishing specialist services (often as a thinly disguised cost-cutting exercise).

CASE STUDY 7.3: PATIENT CHOICE

One of the key aspects of *Equity and Excellence* was also said to be patient choice and satisfaction. Clearly, even the least sophisticated understanding suggests choices must be bounded by issues of what is clinically effective (and, in a publicly funded service, efficient, too). Yet research shows that doctors can be swayed to prescribe antidepressants wrongly or to prescribe particular brands by patients' expressed views [6]. So, understanding of patient choice has to be modified by what the evidence shows about the effects of patient choice, which may sometimes be misinformed. Also, recent funding problems in the NHS mean that there is a deficiency of supply of services, whereas a surplus has to exist if choice is truly to be exercised.

Patient satisfaction does correlate with disease outcomes, and patient-centred care is associated with lower mortality and fewer complications (and, incidentally, higher cost) in at least one study [7]. One of the factors that influence patients' satisfaction is how their requests for services or products are dealt with. This does not mean that requests must be complied with. Rather, it is suggested that responses that respect the patient perspective are most likely to lead to satisfaction [8].

EXERCISE 7.3
Value for money and reducing service expenditure

You may not be part of the NHS but, wherever you are, the service you are running is likely to be subject to changes imposed by politicians, insurers or others who have an interest in securing 'value for money' or simply in reducing expenditure. Can you think of any examples similar to those discussed earlier where too simplistic an understanding of a 'top-down' imperative could lead to negative effects? What evidence can you muster to counteract this possibility? If this is important, can you develop a strategy to communicate this information and to ensure that negative effects are minimised?

In this context, it is also worth considering that the King's Fund investigation into improving the productivity of the health service concluded that *improving clinician performance* through the spread of standardised best practice, not another re-organisation, was the best *evidence-based* way of improving NHS productivity [8].

RISK REDUCTION AND MANAGEMENT

Safety is a key element of quality, and risk reduction is one way of ensuring safety. Doctors tend to focus on clinical risk management. Finance directors focus on financial risk. But there are other risks too. There are risks to reputation and 'brand' if incidents are badly managed, fire risks if regulations are ignored, health and safety risks if people are not properly trained, and so on. Table 7.1 summarises some important areas to be considered in risk management.

In recent years, this kind of systematic approach has contributed to the rapid growth of mandatory training for medical (and other) staff such as information governance, moving and handling, clinical risk, medicines management and educational supervisors' training to name but a few, as well as increased procedures and bureaucracy touching virtually every aspect of day-to-day work as a clinician. It is one of the main complaints that medical staff have raised with one of the authors (SC), namely the ever-increasing paperwork (see also the quotation from Wellington in Chapter 1), form filling and requests for data and information combined with large volumes of emails and numerous automatically generated requests stating the 'information required is now overdue'. Staff feel under pressure. *This in itself can constitute a risk* and the good medical manager needs to do everything possible to reduce unnecessary burden.

The kind of systematic approach advocated in table 7.1 is excellent for an organisation, and it is worth working systematically through this table to ensure all areas are covered.

We don't propose to go into great detail about all the criteria, but we will comment on the principles underlying each of the standards in turn.

Table 7.1 Areas to consider in risk reduction and management

Area	Examples
Governance	Risk management strategy, register, policies, procedures and oversight. Training of managers in risk assessment and management.
Competent and capable workforce	Corporate and local induction, clinical supervision and clinical risk assessment/management training. Management of recruitment and retention.
Safe Environment	Secure environment, issues of over-crowding, moving and handling, safe use and disposal of 'sharps', harassment and bullying.
Clinical Care	Standards and evidence-based practice/guidelines appropriate to clinical areas, record-keeping and communication standards, medicines management, patient involvement.
Learning from Experience	Clinical audit, incident reporting and management, complaints, investigations, analysis, making improvements based on learning, including use of check lists.

GOVERNANCE

This is the way in which the organisation assures itself and others that it has these matters under control (as far as is humanly possible). It takes an overview, ensuring that senior managers are aware of all kinds of risk the organisation faces and that organisational policies and procedures are in place to minimise risk.

COMPETENT AND CAPABLE WORKFORCE

In many ways this could be considered the most important of the standards. Ideally, simply having a fully competent and capable workforce would ensure all the other standards were met. Proper induction to the organisation and to the locality (including locum staff) is clearly vital. Clinical supervision is also vital and the time will surely come when peer supervision, at least, is required for all consultant staff and principals in general practice. Interestingly, when medical audit was first introduced, before it transformed into centralised clinical audit, it did serve the function of peer supervision for consultants and their teams. Training in risk management and good arrangements for CPD and training needs analysis are particularly important when people are being asked to acquire or demonstrate new areas of competency (for example, in the implementation of 'New Ways of Working' – see Case Study 6.2). Training in clinical risk assessment is vital but should not be viewed in too simplistic a way. Experience, general competence in the area under review and detailed knowledge of the patient and his or her condition are at least as important as any of the 'risk assessment' tools currently in use. That is not to downplay the usefulness of such tools whether in assessing risk of pressure sores or self-harm. They are useful and they do remind everybody of the potential risks in particular patient groups, but they are no substitute for proper (multidisciplinary) assessment and judgement by competent clinicians.

EXERCISE 7.4
Applying standards to your service

Choose an area within your sphere of responsibility and use the standards and criteria in Table 7.1 to assess (from your own perspective) the risk in that area related to the workforce. What are the areas of the greatest concern? Who else is (or should be) concerned about these areas? (Together) what can you do about them? When will you do it? (Use the principles of Figure 4.1 to plan actions.)

SAFE ENVIRONMENT

This includes physical risks like needle-stick injuries, moving and handling, and falls. It also includes systemic risks like sickness absence, harassment and bullying, and safeguarding. These are primarily to do with the interpersonal environment.

CLINICAL CARE

The authors would personally want to emphasise the importance (especially in psychiatry, perhaps) of good-quality services and assessments carried out by experienced staff using evidence-based clinical pathways to the list. In an age when an increasing number of initial assessments are made not by senior psychiatrists but by members of other disciplines, it seems particularly important to provide a standardised assessment (we *do not* mean a long form to fill in but an agreed set of relevant information that should be collected – see next section). As much as possible of the standardised assessment should be filled in automatically at referral (eg personal and demographic details, past illnesses and current medication). It is wrong to expect clinical staff to spend time filling in data that can be filled in advance of them ever seeing the patient (though of course, risk management demands they should double-check critical data like allergies). Evidence-based pathways are for guidance. They should leave room for negotiation with the patient and variance based upon the knowledge and experience of the clinician. Standardised pathways reduce the risk of error and make it easier to audit the quality of care, both of which are important risk management objectives. Electronic record systems can be set up to facilitate audit by automatically flagging deviations from the pathway. Remember, though, that a deviation can be for a positive reason as well as a marker of error or omission.

NHS organisations and websites have undergone considerable reorganisation in recent years, and The National Patient Safety Agency, previously an excellent source of useful advice on clinical risk management is no exception. There is now excellent patient safety information at NHS Improvement (www.improvement. nhs.uk). The NHS England website (www.england.nhs.uk) is another great resource. NHS England's aim is to set the priorities and direction for the NHS and to ensure that patients are supported to live longer and more healthily by 'high quality care services that are compassionate, inclusive and constantly improving'. It provides a range of information and resources on all aspects of the NHS for acute and community services, Primary Care and Clinical Commissioning Groups (CCGs) as well as links to other sites such as NHS Improvement. Unfortunately, recurrent reorganisation means these resources often get lost or become difficult to find.

USING CHECKLISTS TO IMPROVE QUALITY

Gawande [9] provides a brilliantly readable description of how he and others worked through the World Health Organisation to devise checklists to improve quality and outcomes in the operating theatre. This was effective in a wide variety of countries and cultures. The process of developing the checklists was an iterative one and was informed by many years of experience about how to develop effective checklists in the aviation industry. There is no space to describe this here, but the book is highly recommended reading for anyone seeking to improve quality and outcomes in healthcare. This is especially relevant when fragmentation of work patterns and pressure of work mean that patients are often transferred from one team to another. Vital information may be lost in the transfer, and a checklist, accompanied by verbal communication, can help to prevent this.

LEARNING FROM EXPERIENCE

Clinical audit

We have given this area its own subheading because we think it is so important and because we think (at least in mental health) it is so badly done. There are two kinds of clinical audit: nationally determined standardised audits which conform to nationally defined criteria enabling comparisons between similar services in different geographical areas; an local audits. Sadly, national audits often do not fully involve the clinicians, and although they provide useful information they only impact on clinical practice indirectly. The Prescribing Observatory for Mental Health in the UK provides a good example of this approach to audit that does have a positive impact on clinicians and services. This is one arm of the Royal College of Psychiatrists College Centre for Quality Improvement (CCQI), [10] which aims to improve standards for users, providers and commissioners of services. As well as coordinating a range of national audits including dementia, antipsychotics and other drugs, the Centre also undertakes work on the Mental Health CQUIN (Commissioning for Quality Improvement and Innovation) and organises a range of accreditation programmes for different mental health services such as the Memory Services National Accreditation Programme (MSNAP). These accreditation programmes have been very successful in improving standards in psychiatry through comprehensive and supportive peer reviews against national standards. As well as being very effective, these accreditation programmes are well respected and highly valued by services. This is in marked contrast to the regime of Care Quality Commission (CQC) inspections, which although much improved compared with 2–3 years ago still cause staff and organisation considerable stress and disruption. These are mentioned as examples. It would be worth visiting the College website for your specialty to familiarise yourself with the relevant information and programmes. Locally determined audits may use nationally agreed criteria or local criteria or a mixture of both. These audits more often directly involve clinical teams and are more likely to have a direct impact on clinical practice. Even these audits have often been taken out of the hands of clinicians, being performed (rather than supported by) audit 'departments'.

We have been involved in locally determined audits where there was a genuine competition between clinical teams to improve standards. We have not seen this with nationally determined audits.

Other criteria for learning from experience

The other criteria speak for themselves. However, we feel that virtually everything that happens is an opportunity for learning. Case conferences and personal reflection on clinical work are obvious examples. Complaints (dealt with in more detail in Chapter 2) are an obvious source of information about things that have (or appear to have) gone wrong. We should also listen to compliments as well as complaints and learn from things that nearly go wrong as well as ones that do.

HEALING WOUNDS

We have added this section because we do not think enough attention is paid to the damage done to organisations by persistent wounds. Complaints, inquiries and other necessary activities are often perceived by staff to be very threatening. After any period of trauma to staff, it is well to have a review of how they are left feeling. Clearly if there is blame to be attached and disciplinary action to be taken, this is even more difficult. But once the dust has settled and any appropriate action has been taken, it is time to draw a line and evaluate the current situation. Persistent resentments and criticisms help nobody. They should be dealt with. One is reminded of the 'truth and reconciliation' movement in South Africa! This sought to heal the wounds of the apartheid era by bringing the truth into the open on the understanding that acknowledging past mistakes without persecuting the perpetrators was essential to enable the country to put the pain of the apartheid era behind it and make a new start.

REFERENCES

1. Department of Health (2010) *Equity and Excellence: Liberating the NHS.* www.gov.uk (accessed 7 January 2018).
2. NHS England (2014) *The Five Year Forward View*, NHS England. www.england.nhs.uk (accessed 7 January 2018).
3. Sackett D, Richardson S, Roenberg W and Haynes R. (2011) *Evidence-based Medicine*, 4th ed. London, UK: Churchill Livingstone/Elsevier.
4. Roberts N, Curran S, Minogue V, Shewan J, Spencer S and Wattis J (2010) A pilot study of the impact of NHS patient transport on older people with dementia. *International Journal of Alzheimer's Disease*, 10: 1–9.
5. Wilkinson R and Pickett K (2010) *The Spirit Level: Why Equality Is Better for Everyone.* London, UK: Penguin Books.
6. Paterniti DA, Fancher TL, Cipri CS, Timmermans S, Heritage J and Kravitz RL (2010) Getting to 'no' strategies primary care physicians use to deny patient requests. *Archives of Internal Medicine*, 170: 381–388.

7. Bechel DL, Myers WA and Smith DG (2000) Does patient-centered care pay off? *The Joint Commission Journal on Quality Improvement*, 26: 400–409.
8. Appleby J, Ham C, Imison C and Jennings M (2010) Improving NHS productivity: More with the same not more of the same. London, UK: The King's Fund. https://www.kingsfund.org.uk/sites/default/files /field/field_publication_file/improving-nhs-productivity-kings-fund-july -2010.pdf (accessed 1 May 2018).
9. Gawande A (2011) *The Checklist Manifesto*. London, UK: Profile Books.
10. College Centre for Quality Improvement (CCQI), Royal College of Psychiatrists. http://www.rcpsych.ac.uk/workinpsychiatry /qualityimprovement.aspx (accessed 7 January 2018).

8

Innovation

INTRODUCTION

Organisations must adapt to changing circumstances. This means being willing to lead and manage necessary change. Other kinds of change, including those driven by political and economic forces and ideology, may be imposed on a medical profession that is often, to say the least, sceptical about such imposed change. Nevertheless, whether change comes from inside the organisation or is imposed from outside, standing still is not really an option. Change must be managed, even if the aim of management is only damage limitation.

Innovation means doing new things, or doing old things in new ways. Doing new things is essential because technology and society change. Many of the classes of medication and types of surgery we use today were not available even 20 years ago. The increasing population (especially of old and very old people) has increased demand in many areas of healthcare. But innovation can be risky and sometimes fails. Failing to innovate also carries risks. Of course, risks can often be anticipated and managed, and there are many systems designed to do this. A good example would be the regulation of new medications to ensure they are effective and as safe for patients as possible before they come to market. Such systems are not without costs; but few of us would want to do without them.

Innovation needs to be led and managed and, in business, the people who do this are often characterised as entrepreneurs:

'...the nature of innovation is that it is fundamentally about **entrepreneurship**. The skill to spot new opportunities and create new ways to exploit them is at the heart of the innovation process.' [1]

The Oxford dictionary defines the entrepreneur in a limited way:

'a person who sets up a business or businesses, taking on financial risks in the hope of profit.'

However, in healthcare, *social innovation and enterprise* [1] is particularly important. Social innovation, in the way the term is used by Bessant and Tidd, is motivated by a vision of social need and a desire to produce social good. The primary concern of social entrepreneurs is creating *social value* rather than *personal profit*.

Particular leadership and management skills and qualities are needed to facilitate innovation. Individuals or teams of individuals who lead and manage innovation in business often rejoice in the title of 'entrepreneur'. Many in the public sector are less comfortable with this label. Although they share many skills and qualities with entrepreneurs in business, their emphasis on creating social value rather than personal profit makes them uneasy with the term.

Whether in the public or private sector, organisational culture (Chapter 3) can facilitate or inhibit innovation. The 'club culture' (as described by Handy [2]), that often dominates government, generally only promotes innovation consistent with its own ideology. The 'role culture' deals well with tasks that can be standardised and 'mechanised'. It is risk averse and tends to lack creativity and resist change. The team culture, found in some senior management and clinical teams in healthcare, strikes a balance between standardisation and creativity. Clinical teams work at this, adapting evidence-based knowledge and guidance from organisations like the National Institute for Health and Care Excellence (NICE) to co-create individual responses to clinical problems. Finally, the 'existential culture' is traditionally the culture of the professional, often working in a loose partnership with other individuals as doctors, barristers, psychotherapists and others have traditionally *practiced*. People in these cultures are often at least as interested in professional standards as they are in the organisation they work for. They often innovate but tend to resist innovation thrust on them from the organisation.

Innovation can be a messy business with missed opportunities and false starts, especially in an organisation as diverse and subject to political interference as the NHS. That is why leadership on an individual and team basis is essential. In this chapter, we will look at the characteristics of people and teams that strive to create social value, at what motivates creativity, and at the process of innovation, illustrated by a variety of case studies of notable innovations relevant to healthcare. We will conclude with a plea for more enterprise and innovation led by medical managers working together with other management colleagues.

ENTREPRENEURSHIP

Creativity is central to social entrepreneurship. This creativity may be expressed in many ways, for example, developing a new medication or a new way of administering it, developing a new design for a hip replacement, designing a service according to new principles (or adopting principles from another area) and so on. Although the concept of entrepreneurship comes from the business world and, in that context is often characterised by risk-taking in the interest of profit, in the health context, social entrepreneurship motivated by a desire to create social value is more important. Peter Drucker, an early advocate of business entrepreneurship, writing from an American perspective went so far as to argue that public service activities should be converted into profit-making enterprises [3]. This is a conclusion with which the authors profoundly disagree, believing that creating social value is more important than creating financial gain. We hope the illustrative examples we have chosen will demonstrate how entrepreneurship in healthcare is more often motivated by a desire for social good than financial return.

Four key characteristics of the entrepreneur can be summed up as

- Creativity
- An open mind
- Careful observation
- An ability and willingness to follow through

Often entrepreneurship involves a team and the leader must be able to inspire the team. Occasionally, as in the discovery of penicillin discussed below, there is a considerable time lag between an initial discovery and the entrepreneurship needed to turn it into a practical, world-changing reality.

WHAT MOTIVATES CREATIVITY?

At the fundamental level, the answer is simply – survival. The human quality of creativity, *coupled with the ability to co-operate* for the common good, is what has enabled humanity to thrive and dominate the planet (as well as producing some distinct threats to our future survival). In capitalist economies, the survival and prosperity of the business often depends on innovating more successfully than competitors.

In healthcare, *social innovation and enterprise* [1] is especially important. As discussed earlier, it is motivated by a vision of social need and a desire to produce social good. The primary concern of social entrepreneurs is creating *social value* rather than personal profit. Successful social innovation depends on a disciplined and organised process to turn ideas and opportunities into reality. It demands the same focused and determined drive as entrepreneurship in the commercial world, even if the motivation is very different. Social innovation is important in healthcare, and case studies later in this chapter can be seen primarily as examples of successful social innovation.

TYPES OF INNOVATION

Innovation may involve new *products* or *processes* or shifting products or processes into new *contexts*. The introduction of penicillin as a widely used antibiotic involved both the product (penicillin) and the development of new fermentation processes to produce it on a large scale. The development of the Virginia Mason Production System (VMPS) for healthcare discussed below involved a careful adaptation of the Toyota Production System (TPS) to the healthcare context, essentially a new application of process innovation. A *paradigm shift* with changes in the underlying mental model of how health services are provided provides another form of innovation, and the launching of the British NHS in 1948 was a powerful example of this as is the smaller social enterprise of NAViGO, also described below.

THE PROCESS OF INNOVATION

Bessant and Tidd [1] provide a four-stage model of the creative process:

- Recognition/preparation
- Incubation
- Insight
- Validation/refinement

Our first case study (Case Study 8.1) looks at an unusual but vitally important piece of entrepreneurship and innovation in medicine: the development of penicillin.

Penicillin

CASE STUDY 8.1: THE DISCOVERY OF PENICILLIN

Most people know the story of how Alexander Fleming discovered in 1929 that the *Penicillium* mould, which had 'contaminated' a culture dish, inhibited the growth of bacteria; but few realise that in 1900, a German scientist had devised the concept of a 'magic bullet' which could kill harmful microbes without significant damage to the host organism. Fleming initially saw the mould as a way of distinguishing between microbes but did not immediately realise its potential as a 'magic bullet' for treating infection. Despite an early successful attempt to use penicillin to treat infection, its further development waited till 1939. By then Howard Florey, Ernst Chain and colleagues at Oxford were exploring the potential production and use of penicillin to fight infections in human patients. Initial success in one patient was unfortunately followed by the patient's death when the limited supply of penicillin they had been able to produce ran out. Florey and a colleague, Norman Heatley, travelled to the USA as large-scale production of penicillin seemed impossible in war-torn Britain. Through academic contacts, they secured introductions to Robert Thorn in the US Department of Agriculture. He, in turn, put them in touch with the Department's Northern Regional Research Laboratory, which had expertise in growing fungal cultures. With support from Heatley, production was rapidly scaled up whilst Florey tried to interest pharmaceutical companies in production and others searched for more easily cultured

(Continued)

CASE STUDY 8.1: (Continued) THE DISCOVERY OF PENICILLIN

varieties of the *Penicillium* mould. Eventually another friend of Florey's, Alfred Norton Richards, swung government support behind the project and a number of pharmaceutical firms began working together. The first 11 US patients were treated between March and June 1942, and the results were encouraging enough for industrial production to be ramped up. With the encouragement of the US government, production was stepped up from 21 billion units of penicillin in 1943 to 6.8 trillion units in 1945. This was a truly staggering achievement and a significant contribution to the war effort. The antibiotic era was born. (For a fuller account, on which this is partly based, see https://www.acs.org/content/acs/en/education/whatischemistry/landmarks/flemingpenicillin.html).

In this example, the four key entrepreneurial characteristics of creativity, open-mindedness, observation and perseverance and follow-through were demonstrated, though by different people. The process of innovation stretched out over quite a long time frame. Ehrlich's idea of the 'magic bullet' was, in Bessant and Tidd's four-stage model, the *recognition* of the problem. Fleming's observation on the antibacterial action of a mould was part of the *preparation* for the Oxford group's *insight* into the potential significance of applications of the observation. The *validation and refinement* stage was much accelerated by the pressures of war and the entrepreneurial activity of the Oxford group, greatly assisted by the industrial might of the USA.

This example is also important for a variety of other reasons. The role of the academic community in innovation is clear from the way in which Fleming's original published findings (and Ehrlich's concept of the 'magic bullet') inspired Florey and colleagues to conduct further research and development. It is also evident in the way that Florey's academic contacts in the US helped him find the right collaborators and swing state support behind the commercial production of penicillin (a positive example of club culture in action). Interestingly, Florey did not attempt to patent penicillin, believing it would be unethical to do so. However, commercial interests did, later, patent penicillin derivatives and production methods. Finally, the extraordinary speed with which this product was developed was a result of collaboration between the US government and commercial interests facilitated, like much medical innovation, by the pressures of war. Another notable example of innovation in war was the development of burns treatment and plastic surgery for Second World War pilots [4]. The inauguration of the British NHS, our second case study of innovation and entrepreneurship, was also facilitated by the Second World War and its aftermath.

The inauguration of the NHS is a good example of paradigm innovation, based on socio-political considerations.

The NHS

CASE STUDY 8.2: THE NHS AS SOCIO-POLITICAL INNOVATION

Although Aneurin Bevan, a Labour MP, is remembered as the founder of the NHS in 1948, the seed had been sown in the years before the 1939–1945 war, when he was chair of the Tredegar Medical Aid Society, which covered 95% of the local community. He had an ambition to extend this kind of cover to the whole UK population. The Emergency Medical Service in the Second World War proved that a centrally organised service could do a great deal to cope with massive civilian casualties (London alone had over 17,000 killed and many more injured). People were looking for a better life after the war and a leading Liberal politician produced the Beveridge report in 1942, promising to tackle 'Want, Disease, Ignorance, Squalor and Idleness'. After the war, with a Labour government in power, the welfare reforms advocated by Beveridge were brought forward and Bevan was responsible for implementing the National Health Service Act. From the start, he was determined that it should be available to all according to need, free at the point of use and (after considering other options carefully) funded from general taxation.

The NHS, as set up in 1948, was tripartite. Primary care services – general practitioners, opticians, dentists and pharmacists – were answerable to local executive committees; maternity, child welfare, health visiting, health education, immunisation and ambulances remained the responsibility of the local authority; and hospitals were administered by Regional Hospital Boards, with teaching hospitals retaining boards of governors directly answerable to the Ministry of Health. Despite several structural re-organisations, Bevan's three principles (with the exception of charges for prescriptions, dentistry and opticians' services) were maintained until the 1990 National Health Service and Community Care Act introduced the concept of an 'Internal Market' and the idea of the purchaser–provider split. Over time this has developed into a market opened in 2012 to 'any qualified provider'. Some are concerned that this will lead to further erosion of Bevan's principles and perhaps eventually to an insurance-based system. Nevertheless, the NHS of 1948 has survived for nearly 70 years and is still, despite current funding difficulties, regarded as a bold and largely successful innovation.

A fuller account of the process and difficulties involved in setting up the NHS can be found at https://www.sochealth.co.uk/2017/07/09/people -wait-longer/ on which this account is partly based. Bevan himself wrote about it in Chapter 5 of In Place of Fear [5].

Bevan oversaw a paradigm shift concerning the provision of healthcare which has, to some degree, been adopted in Europe where healthcare is now seen as a *human right* rather than as a commodity to be bought and sold in the marketplace (eg see the debate in the USA: http://www.medscape.com/viewarticle/882360?nlid=116627_425& src=WNL_mdplsfeat_170718_mscpedit_psyc&uac=80181BN&spon=12&impID=1 391800&faf=1). The recognition of the need had happened in the years between the two world wars when the gross inequality of access to healthcare had led to small scale innovations like the Tredegar Medical Society. The Second World War had brought about a general political will for a better society, but Bevan still needed considerable political negotiating skills and determination to carry the reforms through in the face of opposition from many doctors and the Conservative opposition in Parliament.

The introduction of market principles to the NHS, fully realised in the 2012 Act, is itself a paradigm shift innovation (not one with which the authors agree) which partly reverses the 1948 introduction of the NHS as a public service, though Bevan's principles of a universal service, free at the point of use and paid for from general taxation were, for the time being at least, partly preserved.

If the NHS can be thought of as a social enterprise on a grand scale, the opening-up of the provision of NHS services to 'any qualified provider' in the 2011 'reforms', intended to open the way to commercial interests, paradoxically created an opportunity for staff to take over and run parts of the NHS as social enterprises. This was particularly relevant for those Primary Care Trusts (PCTs) that also provided services such as community health services and, in some cases, mental health services. Staff there were given a 'right to request' and, in selected cases, given support to set up social enterprises [6]. Case Study 8.3 provides a brief description of a successful, relatively small, social enterprise: NAViGO, constituted as a Community Interest Company (CIC) providing mental health and associated services in NE Lincolnshire. NAViGO itself represents a paradigm shift in terms of localism.

NAViGO

CASE STUDY 8.3: NAViGO – A SOCIAL ENTERPRISE COMMUNITY INTEREST COMPANY (CIC)

This CIC was set up in 2011 as a first wave 'right to request' social enterprise. Staff, the people using the services and carers were balloted. Nearly three quarters of staff and nearly all service users/carers voted in favour. Many staff voted in favour because they thought the service would be better, more flexible and more responsive under local leadership. The near unanimous vote of people who used the service, pointed to their confidence in and commitment to the innovative way of working already evident in the services, at that stage, directly managed by the PCT.

The former Director of Mental Health Services in the PCT, Kevin Bond, became the first Chief Executive and pursued a vision based on Social Role

CASE STUDY 8.3: (Continued) NAViGO – A SOCIAL ENTERPRISE COMMUNITY INTEREST COMPANY (CIC)

Valorisation [7]. Feedback and ideas from front-line staff and people who use services are supported and developed where possible. The organisation runs all statutory adult mental health, social care and associated services in the area. The culture is one of true co-production and novel designs and models of service have been developed. Despite being a relatively small organisation, by NHS standards, NAViGO has harnessed the enthusiasm of staff and people using the services to develop an impressive range of pioneering services. A full list and description of these services which include family therapy, community support services, transcranial magnetic stimulation (TMS) and an employment training service (Tukes) can be found on their website (http://www.navigocare.co.uk/our-services/).

NAViGO was established as an independent NHS provider accountable to local people and staff. Its local focus and flattened organisational structure contrasted with many NHS Mental Health Provider Trusts, but it remained subject to inspection by the Care Quality Commission (CQC), from which it continues to get good ratings. A membership of over 600 staff and people who use services vote with equal rights, deciding the constitution and other issues such as direction and spending of surplus. The chair is elected by the membership; both staff and service users have a directly elected, paid non-executive director on the board and elected representatives on other committees. The Chief Executive Officer (CEO) is subject to 3-yearly re-approval by the membership. NAViGO is a 'not-for-profit' organisation. Annual surpluses result from an organisation that creates less waste, has higher staff morale and less sickness, provides ancillary services and trades directly with the public via employment and training schemes. These are disposed of by members suggesting and voting for innovations (see below for examples).

In the first 2 years, staff sickness was reduced by more than half. NAViGO has won numerous awards, including overall winner of *The Guardian* 'public service of the year' award in the first year. The employment scheme (Tukes) also runs innovations such as public cafes, public parks, a commercial garden centre and shops. These let the public see people with mental health problems in a positive role and setting. NAViGO is quick to innovate; it set up a specialist eating disorder unit in 6 months. The Transcranial Magnetic Stimulation (TMS) service was set up as an approved research project, at the request of people who used services. Older people's and adult acute services score highly on many quality indicators. NAViGO campaigns on ethical issues such as non-aversive responses to aggression and supports innovative services in both Macedonia and Antigua. Perhaps one downside is that the local Clinical Commissioning Group (CCG), responding to the pressures of politically imposed austerity, has not been able to fund more innovation, despite quality services, value-for-money and innovation.

There are other social enterprises working within the NHS, mostly providing community health services. There are questions as to whether they will survive the latest NHS re-organisation, the so-called Sustainability and Transformation Plans (STPs), which may or may not have room for such relatively small and innovative organisations.

Buurtzorg: Efficiency, innovation and democracy at work

An example from Europe of an innovative model for providing nursing and social care in the community follows.

CASE STUDY 8.4: BUURTZORG, A NEW MODEL FOR COMMUNITY HEALTH AND SOCIAL CARE

The Buurtzorg model has become a high-profile case study of team working in nursing and social care. The company was set up in the Netherlands in 2006 to deliver community care and has grown into 850 teams of nurses delivering care to 70,000 patients in their homes. The model is based on self-management, where teams of nurses make decision about cases and care plans in consultation with each patient. By decentralising case management to teams, the Buurtzorg model apparently offers a 40% reduction in the cost of care and an average of 30%–40% in reduction of contact hours but with these provided by qualified nurses within a work group of 12. Teams make decisions about personal care with the patient; interventions are targeted and have led to a lower rate of admissions into hospitals and residential care homes. Importantly, this democratic model of management is linked to the lower staff absence and turnover. Although Buurtzorg is operating in a profoundly different environment with high welfare funding and teams made up of experienced clinicians, this model of team building, based on Japanese production methods, has been tried with nurses in the 1980s in the UK. What is being proposed here is a re-introduction of team building methods as an alternative to the highly regulated and hierarchical performance management systems that have dominated the NHS.

A discussion about team working and the value of the Buurtzorg model with Clive Morton, Elizabeth Cotton and Antonia Maclean can be found at http://survivingworkinhealth.org/teamworking.

Finally, the *Five Year Forward View* and associated STPs have come up with some ideas that bridge the traditional gap between primary and secondary care. One of these is illustrated in Case Study 8.5.

A proposal for a more integrated system embracing primary and secondary care

CASE STUDY 8.5: THE 'ONION' MODEL OF PRIMARY AND SECONDARY CARE IN OXFORDSHIRE

(Reproduced with the kind permission of David Smith, Chief Executive, Oxfordshire CCG and STP lead for Buckinghamshire, Oxfordshire and Berkshire West.)

The onion model is an initiative being piloted in Oxfordshire, in an attempt to address the following care issues: Delivering appropriate services at scale; Organised around geographical population based need; Delivering care closer to home; A collaborative, proactive system of care; Delivered by a multidisciplinary neighbourhood team; Supported by a modernised infrastructure. The model shows how care can be organised around populations to provide economies of scale, facilitate practices to work together through federations to share resources and share the workload to provide a better service and manage demand.

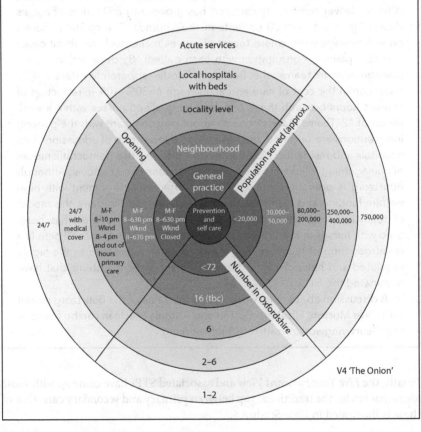

V4 'The Onion'

There have also been a number of other innovations such as *Primary Care Home Initiatives*. These have something in common with the Accountable Care Systems which are the latest format assumed by the STPs. More can be found about them here: https://fabnhsstuff.net/2017/09/25/introduction-primary-care-home/. As yet the ideas are in their infancy and how they will work out in practice, especially in a political climate where the main driver is cutting costs, remains to be seen.

ENABLING CREATIVITY

As discussed earlier, different organisational cultures react differently to entrepreneurial behaviour. Beyond the four 'cultures' described by Handy, other organisational factors can also have an impact. An authoritarian, bullying culture can lead to pressure from higher management and peers to conform, suppressing creativity. Pressure of work can lead to people concentrating on the job in hand and not finding time to imagine better ways of doing things. A 'not-invented-here' mindset can inhibit organisations from adopting new and effective ideas. Management vision like that at NAViGO encourages innovation at all levels to the organisation.

Case Study 8.6 briefly describes another example, focusing on continuous improvement, the VMPS [8], based on the TPS and designed to involve workers at all levels in improving quality and processes and described by many, including Dennis [9].

Virginia Mason production system

CASE STUDY 8.6: THE VIRGINIA MASON PRODUCTION SYSTEM

Virginia Mason (VM) is another not-for-profit healthcare organisation, this time in the USA. Established in 1920, it provided multiple clinics (including what we in the UK would call primary care) and an acute care hospital in Seattle. In 1998 (in common with other medium-sized providers in the USA) it was facing financial problems and questions about the quality of care offered. Management commitment to providing a patient-centred service led to a search for a *management framework, method* or *system* that could deliver both financial soundness and high quality for the patients. A new 'physician compact' that delineated the roles of physicians ('providers' in their vernacular) and the VM organisation was agreed; but they still couldn't find a *management system* in healthcare that would deliver what they wanted. Then they came across the TPS and ambitiously committed to adapting it to healthcare. The TPS was based on eliminating seven types of waste – waste of time, motion, inventory, processing, defects, transportation and

(Continued)

CASE STUDY 8.6: (Continued) THE VIRGINIA MASON PRODUCTION SYSTEM

overproduction. VM management realised that they battled with the same kinds of waste. An example of processing waste might be the writing by clinical staff of long reports that didn't really serve a useful purpose; motion waste might be nurses having to search for materials that should have been to hand for procedures and defect waste had an analogue in doctor's illegible handwriting on prescriptions and so on. TPS had methods for standardising practices to eliminate waste, thus improving efficiency and reducing or eliminating defects in the production of cars (analogous to improving safety in healthcare). Management at VM immersed themselves in the TPS. They trained staff up and established a *Kaizen* Promotion Office (KPO) to act as a resource for continuous improvement in the whole organisations. They used tools adapted from TPS that involved all stakeholders in the design of new facilities and new processes. Rapid Process Improvement Workshops (RPIWs) were used in different areas from surgical operating rooms, to nursing handovers on the wards. Some of the innovations were resisted and when this happened, reasons were sought and innovations modified if necessary. Toyota's famous 'stop-the-line' system that enabled production workers to summon immediate help and, if necessary, halt the production line whilst a potential defect was remedied, was modified to produce a Patient Safety Alert™ System (PSA) which encouraged any member of staff to escalate matters to senior levels if they judged there was a risk to patient safety and encourage a 'no-blame' admission when mistakes had been made. Apart from saving lives, another very measurable result was a 26% decline in professional liability insurance from 2007 to 2008. There is no space here to describe all that has been done and continues to be done through VMPS, but the key point is that this is a *system of management that enables continuous improvement through innovation, mutual respect and the engagement of staff and patients at all levels.*

Effectively VMPS creates a new organisational culture described by Kenney [8] as 'less a fad, more a way of being'. It shares with the NAViGO experience, a conviction about the importance of a vision that is patient-centred and engages staff and patients at all levels in innovation and improvement activity. Its 'unique selling point' is that it is a *system of management* with *thinking tools* that make continuous innovation and improvement part of everyday life. The downside is the amount of time and money invested in training staff and the need for top management who are totally committed to sustaining the processes involved. Both VMPS and NAViGO are not just innovations, but systems or cultures of innovation.

As a spin-off from the VMPS, the Virginia Mason Institute was established to support its implementation in other healthcare settings. NHS

Northeast led the way in introducing the VMPS to the UK. Tees, Esk and Wear Valley NHS Foundation Trust has taken the lead in applying VMPS in a Mental Health setting (http://www.tewv.nhs.uk/site/content/GPs-&-Referrers/TEWV-Quality-Improvement/) and there is interesting work in progress in attempting to apply the VMPS to a group of NHS Trusts under the aegis of NHS Improvement (https://improvement.nhs.uk/resources/virginia-mason-institute/).

LEARNING CREATIVITY

Some people will have a predisposition to the kind of creative thinking needed to be an entrepreneur but everyone is capable of creative thinking, and creative thinking techniques can be taught and learned. Indeed, this ability to learn new ways of thinking is foundational to most innovation. The first stage of Bessant and Tidd's [1] four-stage model of entrepreneurial activity is *recognising* the issue and *preparing* to tackle it. Root cause analysis, familiar as an indispensable tool in investigating safety incidents, is useful here. This involves seeking the *root cause* of an incident or other problem by continually asking 'why?' or 'what's behind that?' The root cause is the one we finally arrive at that, if it is put right, will be most influential in solving the problem. It is somewhat analogous to the issue of diagnosis in medicine. Bessant and Tidd [1] cite an example from surgery of a patient arriving late in the operating theatre. The immediate cause was having to wait for a trolley to take them to the operating theatre, but behind that there was an issue of a broken trolley and behind that, the root cause, lack of regular trolley maintenance. (Of course, if the lack of maintenance was due to lack of staff and the lack of staff was due to insufficient funding, the funding might be the root cause.) Techniques such as pattern recognition, divergent (associative) and convergent (focused) thinking can help here. Once the problem is recognised and understood, a phase of *incubation* enables ideas for solutions to occur. Various techniques like lateral thinking [10] are useful here and elsewhere in the process. Unconscious processes sometimes help, too, producing answers in dreams like Kekulé's of the snake swallowing its tail that elucidated the benzene ring structure in chemistry. One of the authors remembers, after his adult son came to stay with a mystery illness, waking up from a dream saying 'Guillain-Barré syndrome'. At this point *insight* had been achieved. The diagnosis proved to be correct (validation) and after a period in intensive care (implementation), the son made a more-or-less complete recovery. The VMPS and similar systems provide tools and processes to facilitate entrepreneurial activity for individuals and, perhaps more importantly in healthcare, for teams. The VM Institute also provides training in VMPS. The VMPS respects the expert knowledge of staff at all levels in the organisation and of the patients who use their services. This culture of mutual respect is also found in NAViGO and is, in the authors' view, essential to maintaining a healthy, innovative organisation.

NOT ALL INNOVATION WORKS

Not all attempts at innovation work. Drucker's belief in privatised services is challenged by the example of the unsuccessful takeover of the management of Hinchingbrooke Hospital. Circle Health, a private company, took over the management in 2011. Private sector management would, it was hoped, find innovative ways to help the hospital out of its chronic debt problem. One innovation was to give staff shares in Circle Partnership which was a minority partner with Circle Holdings as the majority partner in running Circle Health. This is what caused some to see Circle Health as a social enterprise. The idea of increasing staff engagement by giving them a financial stake in the organisation was an innovation for the NHS. Despite early promise of positive change, following concerns over deteriorating standards, Circle withdrew from the project in 2015. They made a loss of approximately £5m on the project and the contract allowed them to withdraw if their losses exceeded £5m. They blamed the unpredictable workload in an acute hospital together with the financial squeeze put on them by the Commissioners. Was this a failure of private enterprise or did it just demonstrate the impossibility of even breaking even when running almost any service under the conditions of austerity being imposed on the NHS? Fortunately, a successful transition back into the public sector was made and the hospital is now run by North West Anglia Foundation NHS Trust.

Circle continues to successfully run private hospitals and treatment centres which provide services to the NHS and maintains an interest in taking over *profitable* NHS contracts; but the double jeopardy of the unpredictability of acute hospital services and reduced or restricted funding proved unmanageable. Similar problems are emerging with many aspects of social care for older people [11].

MANAGING INNOVATION AND CHANGE

A culture that supports innovation and change is vital. A strongly hierarchical structure that imposes change from the top down is not likely to engage the enthusiasm of staff, and staff engagement is vital for good patient care and innovation. A King's Fund report on staff engagement [12] cites six evidence-based 'building blocks' for staff engagement in the NHS:

1. Develop a compelling, shared strategic direction.
2. Build collective and distributed leadership.
3. Adopt supportive and inclusive leadership styles.
4. Give staff the tools they need to lead service transformation.
5. Establish a culture based on integrity and trust.
6. Place staff engagement firmly on the board agenda.

VM, NAViGO and Buurtzorg are examples of organisations that have innovation built in, using, in different ways and to different degrees, all of the six building blocks.

Because innovation and change are intrinsic to life, it is better to manage them than to resist them. The Japanese idea of *kaizen* or 'continuous improvement' is fundamental to the TPS, and to the VMPS derived from it. We always need to be thinking of better ways of doing things. Opportunities abound in new technologies and new ways of working with people. The flattened hierarchy and genuine involvement of staff at all levels and the people who use the services at NAViGO, VM and Buurtzorg mean people are enabled and motivated to explore new ways of doing things to improve efficiency, outcomes and the patient experience.

Good strategic leadership and direction can help create an organisation with the necessary culture to support innovation. Making resources available for new projects, large and small, through any operating surpluses generated in social enterprises or not-for-profit organisations can enable new ideas to be tried out, as at NAViGO and VM. People's individual interests and expertise can be harnessed to develop business cases for new services that can then attract funding (provided it is not artificially constrained by political factors). The individual interests and expertise of psychiatrists and others at NAViGO have led to an impressive array of specialist services for a relatively small organisation, from TMS (a treatment being researched for depression and other conditions) to family therapy and from a specialist eating disorder service to Tuke's employment and training service. Others, such as a scheme to care for people with confusion and physical illness in the community, have failed because the CCG was unable to fund their continuation. The VMPS is a complete management system for continuous quality improvement, though it remains to be seen how well it can be sustained in NHS organisations, given the need for continuous investment in training to enable continuing service development.

Change comes from many sources. One useful acronym used to summarise these is used in strategic planning. It is known as STEP analysis and looks at Social, Technological, Economic and Political drivers for change (Table 6.1). Sometimes the letters in STEP are mischievously rearranged as 'PEST', putting the political first, which has certainly been a problem for the UK NHS. Political imperatives have resulted in repeated and frequent reshaping of the parts into new organisations so that some of the natural resilience of human systems has been eroded. One of the authors worked in essentially the same job but as part of three different NHS Trusts in 3 consecutive years. For those working in politicised health systems, this is an expression of the problems caused by *the locus of control being outside the organisation*. At the time of writing the first edition, *political* forces were imposing massive change on the commissioning side of the English NHS. As we prepare the second edition, further massive changes (again politically driven) in terms of cash-saving 'STPs' are under way on the provider side. On the *economic* side, the proportion of GDP invested in healthcare is probably inadequate, especially given the costs of marketisation. *Social* change is reflected in demographic changes (especially an ageing population) and changing expectations, some of it driven by *technological* change making an ever-wider range of (often expensive) treatment options available.

The *pace* of technological change has been particularly marked in information technology, expressed not only through the Internet but also through technical advances in imaging and other areas. Someone once calculated that the volume of medical literature doubles every 5 years. Even if much of it is not relevant, that kind of exponential change demands effective strategies to ensure that our medical, educational and management practice remains up to date and evidence based. In the words of one writer, we must adapt from strategies designed for coping in an information desert to strategies designed for coping in an information jungle [13]. *Specialisation* is one way of coping with the complexity generated by such rapid expansion in the knowledge base; but without good management this can result in fragmentations of care. *Standardisation* is another way and is the force behind the burgeoning clinical guidelines industry as well as a vital principle in the VMPS discussed earlier.

Standardisation, either in the design of services or in the actual treatment delivered, seems, at first inspection, to mitigate against professional autonomy (and was initially resisted at VM and NAViGO), but this need not be so, provided guidelines remain guidelines and not mandatory instructions.

Assuming that organisations are allowed some continuity and are not broken up for political reasons, how can they best cope with change?

Some change theorists write about dynamic stability. By this they mean that an organisation retains its essential character but makes small, often incremental changes. This is, after all, the natural way – the way of evolution (which seems to have been remarkably successful). The idea of dynamic stability can be compared to riding a bike. It is hard not to wobble if you are standing still. By moving at a reasonable speed, you achieve stability; but go too fast and there is a danger of a crash. If you and your organisation know what you are there for (*purpose*), where you intend to go (*vision*) and how you intend to behave in getting there (*values*), then it will be much harder to deflect you from your objectives. Like a cyclist in a strange land of twisting lanes, you can take a compass bearing on your objective and, whatever the twists and turns of political policy, you can keep on heading for the place where you yourself and your organisation want to be. Pace is important. As noted earlier, too slow and the cyclist falls off. Too fast and there is risk of an accident! True dynamic stability works best in organisations where there is a clear vision, purpose and sense of direction and where all staff and patients are respected, listened to and contribute rather than being 'controlled'.

Further ideas from Kotter [14] help in managing change. He cites eight reasons why organisations fail to change and a corresponding eight-stage process for 'creating' change (Table 8.1). In many healthcare systems, the first of the obstacles to change is not so much complacency as weariness with politically directed change. Nevertheless, establishing a sense of urgency remains important. A word of caution here, though: it is better to establish urgency through *engagement, vision and desire to be better* than through fear, which is used far too often as a motivating factor by lazy managers (as well as politicians and senior civil servants). The guiding coalition is vital but is no substitute for getting general engagement throughout the organisation. Unless you have key people 'on board' you will be 'rowing against the stream'. Communicating

Table 8.1 Eight stages to successful change

Eight reasons organisations fail to change	Eight-stage process of 'creating' major change
1. Complacency (weariness?)	1. Establishing a sense of urgency
2. Failing to create a sufficiently powerful guiding coalition	2. Creating the guiding coalition: a team of sufficiently powerful people with connections
3. Underestimating the power of vision	3. Developing (and involving staff in developing) a vision and a strategy to carry it out
4. Seriously under-communicating the vision for change	4. Communicating the vision using all means, including members of the guiding coalition
5. Allowing obstacles to block the vision (including people, especially senior people, who don't accept it)	5. Empowering broad-based action, getting rid of systems or structures (and occasionally people) that obstruct the vision
6. Failing to create short-term wins	6. Generating and rewarding short-term wins (improvements in performance)
7. Declaring victory too soon	7. Consolidating gains and producing more change
8. Neglecting to anchor changes firmly in the corporate culture	8. Anchoring new approaches by linking to success and development of staff

Source: Kotter, J., Leading Change, Harvard Business School Press, Boston, MA, 1996.

a positive vision for change is important even (perhaps especially) when the change is imposed politically. It is only by having a strong vision for the organisation and its future that (remembering the old idea of 'judo management') the impetus of imposed change can be used to move the organisation in the chosen direction of providing better healthcare.

EXERCISE 8.1
Change in your organisation

Think of some change you want to achieve in your organisation, or think of how you can maintain a healthy organisation, true to its vision and calling during a period of imposed change. Revisit, purpose, vision and values. Consider Morgan's ideas [15] about the 'boundaries' of organisations, changing context, small changes to achieve large effects, living with continual transformation and emergent order and welcoming new ideas! Look at Kotter's eight-stage process and work out how it can be applied in your context. Good luck.

TEAMWORK VERSUS 'COMMAND AND CONTROL' FOR INNOVATION AND QUALITY

One fact that stands out starkly is that 'command and control', top-down management is not leadership. It does not get the best out of staff or the best outcomes for patients. Nor is a slavish following of market principles synonymous with innovation and entrepreneurship. Leadership involves vision but also evoking the creative potential of people in the organisation. When people are treated like things in mechanised, bureaucratic styles of management, their performance is stifled and their creative potential is unrealised. The examples of NAViGO and the Buurtzorg model discussed previously show how more democratic management can spring loose creativity. The VMPS, whilst more traditional in some ways, emphasises the importance of respect for people in effective leadership [16].

CONCLUSIONS

In this chapter, we have looked at issues of innovation and entrepreneurship. We have discussed the importance of motivation and the relevance of *social enterprise* to healthcare innovation. We have looked at the process of innovation and illustrated it by some examples including the technological innovation of penicillin and its production. We have reviewed social innovation from the large-scale innovation of the UK NHS at the end of the Second World War to the relatively small-scale innovation of NAViGO. We have examined how innovation and creativity can be systemically encouraged, citing the VMPS as a potentially replicable example. We have considered how the creativity of individuals and teams can be fostered by understanding the processes involved and showed how attempts at innovation can be doomed to failure by unrealistic expectations and rising (often unpredictable) demand. Finally, we have taken a look at the processes involved in managing change more generally and suggested an exercise in change-management for our readers. Perhaps the most important lesson of this chapter is that to be successful innovation needs to become part of a culture in which there is mutual respect, engagement and willingness to listen (and take measured risks). Top-down authoritarian cultures (like some in the NHS) discourage innovation.

REFERENCES

1. Bessant J and Tidd J (2015) *Innovation and Entrepreneurship*, 3rd ed. Chichester, UK: Wiley.
2. Handy C (1995) *The Gods of Management*, 3rd ed. Oxford, UK: Oxford University Press. (Re-issued London: Souvenir Press, 2009).
3. Drucker P (1985) *Innovation and Entrepreneurship*, reprinted 2015, (p. 227). Abingdon, UK: Routledge Classics.
4. Mayhew ER (2010) *The Reconstruction of Warriors: Archibald McIndoe, the Royal Air Force and the Guinea Pig Club*. London, UK: Frontline Books.

5. Bevan A (1952) *In Place of Fear*. London, UK: Simon & Schuster. (Reissued by Kessinger Legacy Reprints).
6. Addicott R (2011) *Social Enterprise in Health Care: Promoting Organisational Autonomy and Staff Engagement*. London, UK: The King's Fund.
7. Wolfensberger W. (1983) Social role valorization: A proposed new term for the principle of normalization. *Mental Retardation*. 21(6): 234–239.
8. Kenney C (2010) *Transforming Health Care: Virginia Mason Medical Center's Pursuit of the Perfect Patient Experience*. Boca Raton, FL: CRC Press.
9. Dennis P (2015) *Lean Production Simplified*. Boca Raton, FL: CRC Press.
10. de Bono E (2016) *Lateral Thinking: A Textbook of Creativity*. London, UK: Penguin.
11. Humphries R, Thorlby R, Holder H, Hall P and Charles A (2016) *Social Care for Older People: Home Truths*. London, UK: The King's Fund and The Nuffield Trust.
12. The King's Fund (2015) *Staff Engagement: Six Building Blocks for Harnessing the Creativity and Enthusiasm of NHS Staff*. London, UK: The King's Fund. https://www.kingsfund.org.uk/sites/files/kf/field/field_publication_file/staff-engagement-feb-2015.pdf (accessed 24 November 2017).
13. Stewart T (1997) *Intellectual Capital: The New Wealth of Organisations*. London, UK: Nicholas Brealey Publishing.
14. Kotter J (1996) *Leading Change*. Boston, MA: Harvard Business School Press.
15. Morgan G (2006) *Images of Organisation*. London, UK: Sage Publications.
16. Kenney C (2015) *A Leadership Journey in Health Care: Virginia Mason's Story*. Boca Raton, FL: CRC Press.

FURTHER READING

Nonaka I and Takeuchi H (1995) *The Knowledge-Creating Company: How Japanese Companies Create the Dynamic of Innovation*. Oxford, UK: Oxford University Press.

9

When the going gets tough

Vulnerability has become associated with failure.

Professor Marianna Fotaki
Warwick University

One of the great paradoxes of working in the caring professions is that in the current climate many clinicians find it difficult to show the level of care they have for their patients towards themselves. In this chapter we will focus on general practice, but the issues raised about the risks of working as a GP hold also more generally for doctors and other staff groups. *Work and wellbeing in the NHS: why staff health matters to patient care*, a report by the Royal College of Physicians [1], examines the evidence base about staff well-being and urges action not words. Attending to well-being factors, reducing risks and protecting ourselves through activities to deal with stress and maintain physical and mental health are all important. Ultimately, however, we argue that protecting yourself at work rests on building supportive relationships.

THE CONSEQUENCES OF WORKING IN THE CURRENT CLIMATE

Primary care is providing a growing bulk of health and social care services and is experiencing a period of radical reform. We know that in the target-driven sector, intensification of work and budgeting responsibilities will inevitably have consequences on the mental health of staff. A survey conducted on behalf of the mental health charity, Mind [2] reported that 88% of primary care workers find work stressful, leading 21% to develop associated mental health problems, most of whom were taking medication for depression or anxiety.

In 2015 the NHS England chief executive Simon Stevens announced a £5m scheme to improve the health of 1.3m NHS workers, including a specific health initiative for GPs: the NHS GP Health Service (http://gphealth.nhs.uk/), delivered by the Hurley Clinic Partnership.

For doctors and their patients, the realisation that staff members are vulnerable to mental health problems because of the healthcare system within which they work is a disturbing reality. We know that doctors are increasingly vulnerable to burnout and depression – in primary care, 1 in 10 doctors said that work stress has led to suicidal thoughts, with particular groups such as trainee doctors and women GPs most vulnerable to suicide [3].

One of the reasons why the mental health of our GPs is so little discussed is because of the difficulties attached to GPs admitting that they are experiencing distress. From a systemic perspective, the reasons why GPs might be classified as a vulnerable professional group are striking: the push for 7-day-a-week surgeries and new demanding managerial functions to balance budgets and clinical commissioning in primary care. As health and social care services are increasingly coordinated through decentralised structures, the consequences of a poorly funded health and social care system puts the pressure directly onto those GPs sitting on the boards of Clinical Commissioning Groups (CCGs) and Sustainability and Transformation Plans (STPs). At best, the restructuring of how care is delivered puts GP practices on the front line of juggling financial and clinical demands which increasingly cannot both be met; at worst, this presents a major mental health threat to staff.

This has inevitably had an impact on the numbers of doctors working in general practice with a new £2m training and recruitment fund being created to encourage retired GPs to cover on-call and weekend work. Although both the NHS GP Health Service and attempts to retain GPs are welcome, in 2017 74% of GPs reported to the BMA that their workload was unmanageable, meaning that whatever the policy response, doctors will continue for some time to be functioning under unacceptable working conditions.

RESILIENCE AND WELL-BEING

The debates about workplace well-being and resilience are both fascinating and important. Although mindfulness and specific physical health initiatives can offer welcome techniques for building well-being, there is a growing body of critical research about the use of well-being and resilience initiatives in the current healthcare climate. These critiques rest principally on the argument that the simplistic use of techniques to manage well-being, particularly to help staff self-regulate their emotions, ultimately individualises collective and systemic workplace problems that should be addressed by employers. The claim is that inevitably employers will find it easier, and often cheaper, to train staff to practice mindfulness techniques than deal with external issues such as overwhelming workloads or bullying at work. For this reason, 'resilience' has become a contested term amongst public sector workers, who have over the last two decades been offered resilience courses during periods of mass redundancies and restructuring. As a result, this focus on individual psychological states in the healthcare context is often regarded with some cynicism by staff.

This is not to suggest that well-being initiatives should be avoided, but it does suggest that to make real changes in building well-being, a much broader working definition needs to be used that looks at the internal and external risks and protective factors at play. There are a lot of well-being and resilience measurements that are similarly contested. Some argue that these measurements are reductive, focusing on internal states of mind and leading to an unhealthy sense of ourselves, what has become known as the 'quantified self' [4] where we either pass or fail. Other measurements take a broader approach, looking at both internal and external factors that affect mental health and the balance between them, accepting that all of us work within imperfect systems. Some well-used measurements are the Warwick-Edinburgh Mental Well-being Scale (WEMWBS) and the New Economic Foundation's Five Ways to Wellbeing. Both measures emphasise the importance of being able to make emotional contact with the people around us and to form relationships based on trust. Exercise 9.1 gives you an opportunity to examine risk factors and protective factors in your own workplace.

EXERCISE 9.1
Measuring your well-being

Using Table 9.1, this exercise aims to help you get a perspective on your levels of well-being. This is not a test with defined psychometric properties. It is a way for you to get an overview of the balance between risks and protective factors at play in your life and help to identify some immediate areas that you might want to address. This exercise is best done quickly, allowing you to respond honestly to the statements in column three. Take some time at the end to reflect on what has come up. On the basis of your responses to the questions, think about three things that you could do in the short term to reduce your risks or increase your protections.

Created by www.survivingwork.org.

Table 9.1 Assessing risk and protective factors in your work situation

Factor	Agree 0 = not at all 5 = very much	What this factor means
Risk factors (anything that reduces your capacity to adapt and cope)		
Work (0–5)		• I cannot cope with my workload. • I don't have much control over how or what I do during the working day. • I regularly overwork.
Management (0–5)		• I'm being bullied by a colleague. • I don't trust my SMO. • I am concerned about levels of patient care.
Skills (0–5)		• I don't have the up-to-date clinical skills I need. • I don't understand the online technologies and database we use. • I feel I've lost skills over the last 5 years.
Vulnerability (0–5)		• I am anxious at work. • I am being discriminated against at work. • I feel tearful a lot.
Loss (0–5)		• A patient recently committed suicide. • My department is being cut. • I am concerned about redundancy.
Health (0–5)		• I have a health condition which is getting worse. • I feel tired all the time. • I'm obese.
Relationships (0–5)		• I get into arguments easily. • I find it hard to make emotional contact with the people around me. • I'm lonely.
Neighbourhood (0–5)		• My neighbourhood is dangerous. • Services are limited where I live. • I am isolated at home.
Coping (0–5)		• I drink too much. • I feel numb most of the time. • I go to the gym every day.
Total risk score Maximum score 45		
Protective factors (anything that raises your ability to adapt and cope)		
Work (0–5)		• I believe in what I'm doing. • I like what I do. • I am able to develop and learn at work.

(Continued)

Table 9.1 (*Continued*) Assessing risk and protective factors in your work situation

Factor	Agree 0 = not at all 5 = very much	What this factor means
Relationships (0–5)		• I have someone I can rely on at work. • I socialise regularly. • I feel loved by someone.
Confidence (0–5)		• I am good at what I do. • My work makes a difference. • I like who I am.
Hope (0–5)		• I think the structural problems at work can be addressed. • I think that my team is capable of addressing problems head-on. • I am motivated to keep going.
People (0–5)		• I am able to talk to people about difficult issues at work. • I am able to challenge management decisions. • People trust me.
Learning (0–5)		• I went on a continuing professional development (CPD) course over the last 12 months. • I learned something that I use in my work within the last year. • I know what I want to learn next.
My feelings (0–5)		• I am able to make emotional contact with other people. • When I'm happy, I let people know. • I can cope with getting angry.
Neighbourhood (0–5)		• I feel like a part of the area where I live. • There are things I'm interested in going on in my community. • I feel safe.
Coping (0–5)		• I have something I enjoy doing which does not involve work. • I can avoid drinking or taking drugs when I'm feeling bad. • I can call someone when I'm in trouble.
Total protective score (maximum 45)		

RELATIONALITY IS KEY

One of the proposals of this book is that the key protective factor for well-being and resilience is our ability to form relations with the people around us, for both psychological and organisational reasons. Psychologically, we know that being able to talk about how we feel and our experiences at work with people we trust is crucial to managing stress at work. Whether this is done through a chat over lunch or a BMA training course, we know that finding support from colleagues is key.

Organisationally, the ability to talk openly with colleagues is often underestimated. Firstly, the ability to raise questions and concerns with colleagues is essential for patient safety, something that is underlined repeatedly in the health management literature. When doctors are not able to communicate with other staff members, patient care and safety can be put at risk. Secondly, most people are not able to create meaningful changes in their working conditions on their own. It is almost always through raising issues with colleagues, both formally and informally, that organisational problems can be looked at rather than buried or denied (Box 9.1).

BOX 9.1: Surviving work in healthcare (www.surviving workinhealth.org)

Surviving Work in Healthcare is a free resource designed to provide an accessible entry point for key workers and front line managers to survive work. The resources include a series of conversations between senior practitioners, brought together to ask practically how can people survive working in healthcare? Resources cover 10 themes:

1. *Bullying at work*: Why healthcare has a culture of bullying and why we are all involved.
2. *Healthy organisations*: What makes workplaces sick and why we can't stop getting ill?
3. *Understanding healthcare*: What are the systemic factors that shape healthcare delivery?
4. *Precarious work*: The realities of working conditions and wages in healthcare.
5. *Precarious workers*: What happens to us when we work in precarious jobs?
6. *Dynamics in groups*: Why does working with other people make us anxious?
7. *Racism*: Why does discrimination happen every day in healthcare?
8. *Managing healthcare*: How to manage dysfunctional teams and survive the process.
9. *Team working*: Why team working is the only show in town.
10. *Solidarity in healthcare*: How to make friends and influence people at work.

These resources take a jargon-free, de-stigmatising and practical approach for addressing the real problems of working in healthcare.

MENTAL HEALTH FIRST AID

It is an obvious point that if you are working under stress, you are likely to be affected; so one of the first things to establish is whether you are able to function responsibly at work. Often anxiety and strong feelings such as anger can be provoked very quickly, especially if we are depleted and under pressure. Mental Health First Aid provides some simple and immediate techniques to take control of your anxiety or feelings of distress at work. There are different techniques that people can use to help restore our capacity to work, but in the next box we have a simple five-stage approach which we are calling CABIN, developed by www.survivingwork.org, working with healthcare workers (Exercise 9.2) to help restore self-regulation. In the cold light of day this might look patronising, but it is helpful to prepare some techniques you can use quickly in a situation of high stress.

EXERCISE 9.2
CABIN

Contain: Remove yourself from whatever is making you anxious and find somewhere where you feel safe. If you can, call a friend or find someone at work you trust to help you.

Acknowledge: Do not try to ignore what has just happened. Acknowledge the anxiety you are feeling.

Breath: Try to control your breathing, lengthening your breath and, if it helps, count one-two-three slowly in your head. Keep going until your breathing has normalised.

Identify: Work out what you are worried about right now. Focus only on the immediate cause of stress.

Next steps: Work out what the next steps should be in the short and longer term. This stage is always better if you can find a friend to do this with.

Probably the most effective way of reducing anxiety is to contact a friend or someone you trust at work and ask them to help you. When you are anxious you are unlikely to be thinking straight, so find a time when you are relatively relaxed and think through who you would call and make sure you have their number on your phone.

If someone comes to you with a problem that is making them anxious, it is important to let them speak and to listen without interrupting or correcting them. On one level anxiety is a problem of misperceiving reality, but by pointing this out you are unlikely to help anyone feel less anxious. What is important is that you acknowledge they are feeling anxious and gently help them to think about what they can do next.

SUPERHEROES AND SUPER-EGOS

One of the difficulties of talking about doctors' mental health is how to manage the tension between the defences needed to work with patients and being realistic about the mental health problems that doctors are vulnerable to. For many doctors there is a profound nervousness in acknowledging vulnerability and mental health problems, and in many cases they will be unaware that they are living with mental illness. This reluctance is actively encouraged by the demands for certainty, treatment and targets now expected of doctors. There is no room within this system for the clinician to be unsure, make mistakes or underperform. For GPs working with the system of many short appointments in a day, it is not hard to understand why they are reluctant to touch upon their own distress.

There is a growing acceptance that one of the occupational risks for doctors is how to maintain a balance between having a strong ego and sense of their own capacities and the specific need for doctors to have a sense of their own limits and need for care. Putting it bluntly, many people driven by vocation, with high intellectual and educational achievements, can become unrealistic about the natural limits we all operate under. There is inevitably a fine line between having a strong ego and creating a 'super-ego' that makes punishing demands on the clinician to work heroically under unsustainable conditions. Coaching and mentoring can help to avoid the 'superhero syndrome' (see Chapter 5).

The nature of the profession and training process attracts people who are driven and make high demands on themselves. Although having a strong sense of your capacities is necessary, when this version of the self goes unchecked, it can easily lead to unrealistic expectations and 'omnipotent' fantasies about what can be achieved at work. This 'superhero' tendency places unsustainable demands on the clinician and results in experiences of shame for those doctors who are not able to cope. This shame is a major block in doctors finding help and addressing problems before they develop into long-term problems such as burnout or serious mental illness.

Additionally, doctors who are unrealistic about their own health can become emotionally defended as a way of protecting themselves from psychological stress. Exposure to distress is inevitably part of the job; but when clinicians' coping strategies result in them becoming cut off from their own feelings, they inevitably become cut off from their patients, as well as undermining self-care. This inappropriate degree of detachment is in contrast to the appropriate detachment discussed in Chapter 5. In order to provide good care, you have to care about both your patient and yourself.

For people trained to build relationships with their patients, there is something paradoxically hard for many doctors about building relationships at work. This is in part due to the highly competitive nature of the training – encouraging often highly individualistic and self-sufficient ways of functioning and a reluctance to face up to personal needs and vulnerabilities.

It is also a common defence in stressful jobs to manage feelings of anxiety and conflict by withdrawing from other people. Avoiding staff meetings and the staff kitchen are really common ways that people insulate themselves from being exposed to difficulties and conflict at work. This can become another inappropriate defence where retreating from contact with others leads to people becoming cut off from the very people that can support them at work. Box 9.2 records a conversation between two doctors with many years' experience in general practice.

BOX 9.2: An honest conversation between two doctors

Chris: I'm not wishing to say we're trained badly, I think we're trained inadequately. I don't think we're prepared for the distress and the amount of work that's expected of most people going into healthcare. The distress that has to be held – the fact that it's recognised we need Schwartz rounds and Balint Groups. Psychotherapists, psychologists and psychiatrists can hold the distress they hold because they are in regular supervision. There is a lightening conductor for people working with distress in certain professions and not others and that seems to me to be a big hole in how we treat doctors. We're now recommending self-care for the general public and I think we now need self-care in the curriculum for doctors. We are wired firstly as people not as doctors – these things become part of our being, they may be thrust upon us and part of expectations of our families, even before we're born.

Clare: We're here in the Tavistock Clinic which ran a whole series of seminars called Beyond Balint – run by Gerhard Wilke who is a group analyst and anthropologist and what he argues is that what general practice is now suffering from is the bereavement of the doctor-patient relationship being the most important relationship we can have in healthcare. Even that has fallen apart. We now have the 'third eye' in the consulting room – that's the commissioner. How much are you spending? Where are you referring patients? General Practice has become both the scapegoat and saviour. Everything that's gone wrong in England is our fault – from climate change to the price of oranges. But we're also the saviours – GP led NHS, GPs running commissioning groups, go and see your GP. Being the saviour and the scapegoat does not sit well with individuals who just want to help their patients.

Chris: As if the job wasn't enough, it's all the things doctors are expected to do around commissioning – being all things to all people and having all capabilities and competences – nobody ever thinks about capacity. Part of this is increased patient expectations and the politicians who encourage those expectations and make the job impossible.

Clare: But most of it is that there's no real interaction between us – patients and doctors, doctors and other doctors – its the relationship between you and me that makes the difference.

Chris: This is one of the arguments about resilience. There are lots of resilient people around in this country, they're running it and running lots of people into the ground. I don't want resilience when I go and see a doctor I want caring and I want that person to be able to be healthy in themselves and supported. The greater the distress the more we need it. We can't hold other people if we're not in a position where we can hold ourselves.

This conversation between Clare Gerada and Chris Manning can be viewed in full on http://survivingworkinhealth.org.

PROTECTING YOURSELF AT WORK

The nature of a doctor's work makes it even more important that you work in a way that offers you some level of emotional protection. Here are some immediate steps you can take.

Start where you are

For many people working in healthcare, there is a disorientation about the systems they are working in and a denial about how they feel about it. It is a natural defence against disappointment to pretend that things are better than they are and to deny the problems we may be confronted with. One of the reasons for this is that looking realistically at our working lives requires a level of 'ordinariness' and accepting that our working lives are not perfect and often problems do not have obvious or complete solutions. It also often means confronting difficult emotions, such as anger, and being able to manage them sufficiently to continue to function at work. This is complex for doctors because although we might be very good at dealing with our patients' emotions, it is inevitably much harder to deal with our own. However, in order to really understand our own states of mind, we have to be able to look honestly at how we feel.

When we try to suppress or deny our emotions we can fall vulnerable to adopting toxic coping strategies which can range from using alcohol or drugs, to burying ourselves in work. Addictions function to help us cut off emotionally as a way of managing overwhelming feelings. This is particularly the case with overwork, which most doctors do not address because it is a 'socially acceptable' defence and often encouraged by workplace cultures. However, inherent in toxic coping strategies is a paradox in that they actually make us less able to cope over time because they undermine our self-confidence. Addiction involves a series of blackmails that if you challenge the dependency, then you risk losing everything, or at least that is how it feels.

What we do know is that unless we tackle our toxic coping strategies things are likely to get worse, so a key part of protecting ourselves is going to be finding people and services that can help us overcome any bad habits that we have, including burying ourselves in our work.

Setting your limits

The second step towards protecting yourself is to set some boundaries about when and how you work. Establishing a sustainable way of working requires being realistic and accepting that you cannot do everything. Again, it is important to show yourself some compassion here, rather than listening to an internal voice ('critical parent' in transactional analysis [TA] terms, see Chapter 2) which can often moralise or bully us into doing the 'right thing' when it is not right for our well-being. Although there is a real need for doctors to have resilience, the toughness encouraged in a system of targets and administration is not a substitute for good mental health because it denies hard realities of time, resource and emotional limitations.

The main point here is that it is important to stand up to unrealistic demands and to stand firm on what you believe is a sustainable framework for you. This might involve setting a time limit for responding to emails, keeping your private number private, and being explicit about tasks or areas of work that you are not comfortable doing. Although there is a self-protective aspect to setting limits, it is also likely that in order to successfully challenge unrealistic demands, you will need to open up a debate within your workplace with colleagues about how workloads can be managed and addressed.

Getting on with people at work

Most of us want to get on with our colleagues but often find it very difficult to do. Especially in a context of constantly changing structures and services; to maintain communication and understanding with the people we work with presents real challenges.

The reality is that communication between clinicians, especially across disciplines is crucial to good patient care. The research, much of it carried out following the Mid-Staffs scandal, indicates that when we retreat into occupational silos and stop communicating within our teams, more clinical mistakes will happen. The General Medical Council's (GMC's) professional code recognises that doctors have a duty to communicate within teams to ensure quality patient care. Informally, making contact and spending time developing your relationships with colleagues provides an important basis for your work. If we are able to talk honestly and openly with the people we work with, then we create a workplace culture where this level of communication is possible.

Well-used models for medical practitioners are Balint Groups and Schwartz Rounds – both common practice in hospital settings. Both models offer a model of clinical supervision where small groups of clinicians meet on a regular basis to discuss patients and critical incidents at work. Psychiatrists often have peer group meetings as part of their continuing professional development. Groups can be run in any way that best responds to your workplace, but they tend to follow some basic rules:

- Everything said in the group will be treated as confidential.
- Every speaker should be listened to with respect and without interruption.
- Members should be encouraged to disclose whatever they feel comfortable.
- Where possible, next steps for the group should be identified.

It may be that in your workplace there are existing groups including those explicitly focused on providing clinical supervision but also study groups, professional seminars, professional body or trade union meetings. In some cases, it may not be possible to join or create new groups in your workplace; however, introducing these ground rules for team meetings can be one step towards building a collegial and solution-focused culture.

In some cases, informal contact with colleagues can be more powerful in building support at work. Most of us do not spend enough time just talking and listening to colleagues, particularly in workplaces where there is no common area. It means that this everyday communication must be built into our working lives, even when we are already overstretched. Even the simplest interaction – asking how colleagues are and showing an interest in them – can be important in setting the foundations for relationships that are robust enough to survive the challenges in healthcare settings.

Having someone you can rely on

An important but often overlooked step in protecting yourself is to identify key people who you can rely on at work, particularly when the going is tough. You can do this informally or look to establish a formal mentoring relationship or make use of your professional or union memberships. In the main, people respond well to requests for help and often are flattered to be considered a friend and supportive colleague.

The selection of people or organisations is important because they need to be people that we trust and think are on our side. Although most people would like to call on their family and close friends sometimes it can be difficult to know who you can go to. Sometimes, help comes from people that we may not immediately think of. It is important to think about people that you have relied on in the past and what specific help at work you need from them. It is important not to discount asking for help just because you are not closely connected on an emotional level. Box 9.3 summarises the help available from the NHS GP Health Service, which was launched on the 30 January 2017 with The Hurley Clinic Partnership as the provider of this service. The service is self-referral only for GPs and GP trainees in England.

BOX 9.3: NHS GP Health Service (England)

Confidential Helpline: 0300 0303 300
www.gphealth.nhs.uk

WHAT DOES THE SERVICE LOOK LIKE?

- It is a free, confidential service provided by health professionals specialising in mental health support to doctors.
- It is accessible via a confidential national self-referral phone line, website and app, enabling GPs and GP trainees to seek information about the services available, access self-help tools, and access clinical support.
- Treatment services are available in all 13 localities across England, with local delivery supported through a local lead.

(Continued)

BOX 9.3: (Continued) NHS GP Health Service (England)

- There is a range of clinical support, accessible across England, with GPs and GP trainees free to choose the most suitable locality which matches their needs.
- There is a choice of different premises across local services to enable ease of access, with the confidence of anonymity to minimise risk of meeting colleagues or patients.

WHERE ARE THE SERVICES TO BE LOCATED?

The services are available within each of the 13 NHS England local team areas. Within each area there is a network of clinicians which can be accessed at a range of different sites and clinicians.

WHAT SORT OF SERVICES CAN GPs AND GP TRAINEES EXPECT?

Some examples of the support available through this service are the following:

- General psychiatric support and treatment (face-to-face)
- Support for addiction related health problems (face-to-face)
- Psychological therapies, for example, Cognitive Behaviour Therapy (CBT) (face-to-face or via video technology/call)
- Brief psychotherapy
- Group therapy including reflective practice groups
- Local group addressing specific areas (eg suspended doctors, addicted doctors or specific issues affecting mental health in a particular area)

The service will also signpost GPs to other services where necessary, for example:

- Financial and personal support
- Support in relation to regulatory/performance issues
- Legal/indemnity support
- Support to return to clinical practise

There is no quick-fix measure for protecting yourself at work, and maintaining well-being is an ongoing process throughout our working lives. By its nature, surviving work requires being able to adapt to the complex changes that are happening in healthcare, often suddenly and unexpectedly. The proposal of this chapter has been that protection involves multiple processes including understanding our working environments, managing our risks and protective factors including using a first aid approach in times of crisis and building informal and formal relationships with the people that we work with. This approach to building well-being emphasises relationality and maintaining emotional contact with the people around us as the keys to protecting ourselves throughout our careers.

REFERENCES

1. Royal College of Physicians (2015) *Work and Wellbeing in the NHS: Why Staff Health Matters to Patientcare.* London, UK: Royal College of Physicians. https://www.rcplondon.ac.uk/guidelines-policy/work-and-wellbeing-nhs-why-staff-health-matters-patient-care (accessed 21 October 2017).
2. Mind (2016) *Stress in Primary Care Staff.* https://www.mind.org.uk/news-campaigns/news/mind-finds-worrying-levels-of-stress-among-primary-care-staff/#.WZK3k62ZO9Y (accessed 21 October 2017).
3. Dobson R (2001) Stresses on women doctors may cause higher suicide risks. *British Medical Journal,* 322: 945.
4. Lupton D (2016) *The Quantified Self: A Sociology of Self-Tracking.* Cambridge, UK: Polity Press.

FURTHER READING

GPs

For the NHS GP Health Service, see http://gphealth.nhs.uk.

For information about Balint Groups, see http://balint.co.uk.

For information on Schwarz Rounds, see http://www.kingsfund.org.uk/sites/files/kf/field/field_publication_file/schwartz-center-rounds-pilot-evaluation-jun11.pdf.

For a useful blog and resources by the kind Dr Sunil Rahija, see http://www.drsunil.com.

Psychiatrists

For the Royal College of Psychiatrists, Psychiatrists' Support Service, see http://www.rcpsych.ac.uk/members/psychiatristssupportservice.aspx.

General

For useful health practitioner tips on managing working life, see https://wire.ama-assn.org/life-career/cleveland-clinic-s-approach-burnout-focuses-relationships.

For the BMA Doctors Counselling and Advisory Service, a 24-hour confidential service, see http://bma.org.uk/practical-support-at-work/doctors-well-being.

For some up-to-date research on doctors' health, see the BMA's recent International Conference of Physician Health website: http://bma.org.uk/icph2014.

An interesting social media campaign is #Hellomynameis, which is encouraging doctors to be more emotionally engaged with each other and patients; set up by Kate Granger.

A useful online and face-to-face medical reading group is @TwitJournalClub.

A good individual and anonymous online public mental health service is the Big White Wall: www.bigwhitewall.com.

10

Continuing development in leadership and management

BACKGROUND

The Irish proverb *Every beginning is weak* is especially true, in our view, for those getting started in medical leadership and management. There are a bewildering range of courses, conflicting advice and many different career paths. These will be discussed in more detail in this chapter. This chapter begins with a brief look at some of the key changes in medical education and training in recent years, with an emphasis on the role of the General Medical Council (GMC) and Health Education England, so that the current situation makes more sense. How to identify your training needs and access courses and other ways of learning will also be discussed as well as how to overcome obstacles to training and how to develop your knowledge and skills over time. Some of these will be specific to your role as a doctor, others to more clearly defined medical management roles. Both education and training are important in developing your medical management and leadership skills and these will be explored in more detail, especially ways to review and challenge your progress including peer groups, learning sets, coaching and mentoring to help you achieve your objectives.

CHANGES IN MEDICAL EDUCATION

There have been significant changes in medical education and training in recent years across Europe and the UK. The main change has been a move away from learning large numbers of facts to developing knowledge and skills through a more balanced combination of education and training. There has also been a greater recognition and emphasis on medical leadership at all stages of training in large part because of the importance of medical leadership for substantive doctors working in diverse, ever-changing and complex healthcare organisations. As an illustrative example, the publication of *Tomorrow's Doctors,* initially published in 1993 [1], was a significant step forward for medical student education in the UK. It stressed the need for understanding and core learning rather that an emphasis on rote learning. This welcome change was also implemented in post-graduate medical education. *Unfinished Business* [2] recommended reform of the junior doctor Senior House Officer grade. The 2-year Foundation Programme was started in 2005, followed by the Specialty Training Programme in 2007. This was important from our perspective as the postgraduate curricula, for the first time, emphasised the importance of management and leadership training.

The GMC [3] also provides a helpful framework for doctors in relation to leadership and management development. It covers important topics such as maintaining and improving clinical standards, revalidation, employment issues, recruitment, supervision and the use of resources. The GMC has a crucial role in relation to medical education and training in the UK and sets the standards, approves curricula and monitors delivery. The Medical Royal Colleges produce the curricula and the four Local Education Training Boards (LETBs) in England (Deaneries in Scotland, Wales and Northern Ireland) manage and deliver training.

IDENTIFYING YOUR TRAINING NEEDS

Before rushing ahead and doing lots of courses, it's useful to think about what you want to achieve and, as Stephen Covey [4] suggests, keep the end in mind, as least as far as it's possible. What knowledge and skills do you need for your current role and in the longer term? What are your career aspirations? Make a note of your ideas and discuss them with colleagues, including those involved in medical leadership such as your Medical Director. You could also discuss your ideas as part of the appraisal process, including your reflections and in your Personal Development Plan (PDP). These discussions feed into the job planning process, making it easier for you to achieve your training objectives, especially if there are likely to be significant time and cost implications. You can also do some personal reading, visit websites such as the Faculty of Medical Leadership and Management (FMLM) (see the following), and it's also worth considering undertaking a more formal training needs analysis (TNA), especially if you need to build a case for significant funding and time for study leave. Remember that appraisal and job planning usually take place annually, so your TNA will need to take into account your longer-term needs. There are a number of benefits of undertaking a TNA and some of these are summarised in Box 10.1.

BOX 10.1: Benefits of undertaking a TNA

- Identifies gaps in your knowledge and skills
- Identifies what training needs to be undertaken
- Helps develop a training plan
- Helps to monitor progress against the plan
- Ensures only relevant training is undertaken
- Helps to maximise limited resources (time, staff and costs)

A summary of some of the practical issues to take into consideration when undertaking your own personal TNA can be found in Box 10.2. You can then develop a specific medical leadership and management development plan. For a more detailed guide to undertaking a TNA see [5] as an example. There are also a number of useful resources to help you with ideas, information and training, including the FMLM (www.fmlm.ac.uk) and the British Medical Association (BMA) websites (www.bma.org.uk). Individual medical colleges also have useful information on their websites, so it is also worth checking these for more specialty-specific information. The *Medical Leadership Competency Framework* [6] was first published in 2008 and is an excellent starting point as it describes the competences that doctors in different specialties need in order to be 'actively involved in the planning, delivery and transformation of services'. Your education and training should ideally be a developmental process, similar to the development of clinical knowledge and skills. Each 'stage' of training (eg each year/appraisal period) should be 'mapped' against the 'competences' agreed in your PDP, rather than your training simply being a series of poorly integrated and often random courses.

Although this chapter has focused on the needs of the individual, organisations will often undertake an organisational TNA. It's useful to know what this is as it will help you to align your training needs with those of your organisation. Organisations have limited resources, so depending on current

---

BOX 10.2: Producing your medical leadership and management personal development plan

- Think about your current role as well as potential future roles
- Discuss your ideas with colleagues and especially those in medical leadership positions
- Do some background reading and visit relevant websites
- Use the appraisal process to discuss your ideas, reflect on these and generate a draft PDP
- Use the job planning process to further discuss and agree your PDP, including study leave requirements (time and costs)
- Have the longer term in mind so you can develop a balanced portfolio of knowledge, skills and experience for the future – not just for now
- Take time to think through and agree your training needs and seek professional guidance or a more formal TNA if required. This is preferable to rushing ahead and wasting valuable time and other resources
- Try and align your training needs with those of your organisation for a win-win. This helps enormously when seeking study leave approval
- Consider working with a mentor within your organisation for discussions, reflections and support

issues (eg a recent negative Care Quality Commission [CQC] report), training might have to be prioritised in certain areas during the financial year in question. Being aware of these issues will give you the bigger picture and help in your discussions about funding and other resources to support your development. Organisations have to be fair to all their staff members, and compromises and difficult decisions might have to be made due to limited resources. This emphasises the importance of making a well-argued case if you are seeking funding for an expensive course and/or one with a significant time commitment.

OBSTACLES TO ACCESSING EDUCATION AND TRAINING

It's useful to be aware of some of the obstacles to training as these will help you to plan your training more effectively and overcome most of them. One of the main obstacle is not being clear about what you need, so careful thought and your TNA will help with this. This will help you to focus both in the short, medium and even the longer term. You'll need to have some flexibility and it's useful to review and update your plans and TNA every year or so, for example as part of the appraisal process. The enormous variety of courses can also feel a bit daunting and deciding which course to choose can be difficult. Your TNA will be a great help here and allow you to be more focused and decisive whilst being flexible. Time pressures due to clinical and other work as well as training needs are other important factors, and if you have a lot of outstanding mandatory training, this may make it more difficult to get your study leave approved. Good interpersonal relationships are also crucially important, especially from colleagues who will be asked to cover your clinical work whilst you are away. Everyone is under more pressure these days compared with just a few years ago, so there will need to be some form of reciprocity of cover to keep your colleagues' support, especially if your training will involve lots of time away. Most colleagues are happy to cover a few days, but if you are away, for example 1 day/week for an extended period, this can often lead to friction and needs to be managed sensitively and in advance to maintain goodwill. Other factors include cost and similar resource issues. These can soon rocket if you are likely to be away on a residential course with hotel costs. For some expensive management courses, you might be asked to make a financial contribution or you might need 'special approval' over and above the normal study leave process but this will vary from organisation to organisation, so discussion with the Medical Director or the person appointed to manage postgraduate medical education will be important. Support from your organisation is more likely if you are clear why you want to do the course, if the course doesn't require a lot of resources (time and costs) and the training is aligned with the needs of the organisation. See Box 10.3 for a summary of these points.

BOX 10.3: Obstacles to education and training

- Not being clear what you want to do or need now (and in the future), causing a lack of focus
- The large number and variety of learning opportunities, making choice and focus more difficult
- Choosing the most appropriate type of learning activity, for example, specific skills-based training (negotiating skills, media training), learning sets, peer groups, mentoring, coaching and different courses such as day release and Master's degree in Business Administration (MBAs) (see Chapter 5)
- Location, duration and cost of training
- Work-related pressures
- Demands of other training, including mandatory training
- Limited time and funding available for study leave
- Persuading colleagues to cover your routine work
- Not making best use of the appraisal and job planning processes
- Not aligning your training needs with your organisation's corporate and service-level requirements

---

TYPES OF EDUCATION AND TRAINING AVAILABLE

There is no doubt that leaders are needed in the healthcare sector and this has been emphasised by Bagnall [7], who looked at some of the facilitators and barriers to leadership and quality improvement. The study was relatively small and focused on junior doctors but concluded that the future of leadership needs debate and the NHS requires 'well-equipped clinical leaders'. Whilst this is now a widely accepted view, there is less clarity about how doctors should get this training. There are certainly plenty of courses to choose from, including formal qualifications at Certificate, Diploma and Master's levels (see the following). The key issue is which course to choose and this is largely going to be based on your training needs, available time and costs, to name but three. This is a flavour of what is available, rather than being a comprehensive guide as this is a rapidly developing area; it is becoming an increasingly crowded market and the training needs of different individuals will vary. Education and training can be delivered in a wide range of ways including face-to-face, e-learning, other forms of distance learning and, increasingly, as webinars. There are also an excellent range of videos and webinars on YouTube – search for 'medical leadership' (www.youtube. com). They are of varying length and many are from respected organisations on a range of topics such as leadership, competences and developmental programmes and are well worth a look to give you a flavour of what's available. There are also a vast number of courses and organisations delivering leadership and management training for businesses. However, in this section the focus has been aimed specifically at doctors.

Your organisation will probably provide some form of in-house and focused training such as recruitment, managing budgets, managing doctors in difficulty, writing a business case and service transformation. Larger organisations might also have a management and leadership development programme for staff. Have a look at your organisation's intranet page and discuss this with colleagues working in medical management for more details.

Other useful sources of information are the websites of the various Medical Royal Colleges. There is usually useful information about publications and books, relevant documents, courses and links to related sites. For example, the Royal College of General Practitioners has a useful *Leadership Strategy* document (www.rcgp.org.uk) as well as information about courses such as commissioning, practice management and finance. The Royal Society of Medicine (www.rsm.ac.uk) also has some resources relating to leadership and management, including documents and some useful videos.

Health Education England (www.hee.nhs.uk) and similar bodies in other devolved administrations also have a range of resources and courses available. Courses are usually for a full day or a few days over several months and are usually aimed at doctors in training or newly appointed consultants or GPs. One important and exciting opportunity for trainees is the Out of Programme (OOP) scheme. These are for Specialty Trainees and GP Specialty Trainees (GPSTs) and there are several types. There are two options available to develop additional clinical or other experience. Out of Programme Training (OOPT) allows the trainee to gain additional clinical Training experience and these posts needs approval from the GMC. The second option is Out of Programme Experience (OOPE). This programme allows the trainee to gain additional Educational (and/or clinical experience, eg in another country) but these posts do not need approval by the GMC, so there is more flexibility for trainees and allow for more imaginative training opportunities. For example, in Health Education Yorkshire and the Humber (HEYH), trainees can apply for a *Leadership Fellow* post (part of the *Future Leaders Programme*). This provides practical and academic experience for 12 months (full time) in clinical leadership. Trainees are expected to build regional networks with NHS leaders and develop and enhance their skills and competences to prepare them for future medical leadership roles. Trainees are also expected to develop and deliver a specialty or management-focused project that is relevant to the needs of the NHS. For example, in HEYH some Specialty Trainees (STs) in psychiatry have been developing and delivering a training programme for *Recognising and Assessing Medical Problems in Psychiatric Settings* across the region to improve knowledge and skills of physical health for staff (eg nurses and healthcare assistants) working in psychiatry. The programme is now well established and is highly valued by trainees. Leadership development is supported through feedback and reflection, 360-appraisal, coaching, mentoring, presentation skills development and project planning. There is also an annual *National Future Leaders Conference* to bring future leaders together to exchange ideas, experience and projects. OOPEs don't contribute to clinical training, so the date for the Certificate of Completion of Training (CCT) will normally have to be extended by an amount equal to the duration of the OOPE. However, these programmes do provide trainees with valuable additional experience and the potential for some to develop their leadership and management skills.

The BMA website (www.bma.org.uk) is also worth a visit. There is helpful information about specific courses including negotiation skills training, and you can also download the BMA Events app to help manage these. There is also information about more detailed training such as the *Diploma in Medical Leadership and Management* and the BMA *Leadership Programme*. As well as developing leadership knowledge and skills, it not surprisingly also aims to improve your 'political' awareness – not necessarily a bad thing in an increasingly politicised healthcare system. The BMA also has a Medical Managers Committee. This represents the views and best interests of medical managers by acting as an advisory body for the BMA Council on issues relevant to medical management and leadership.

One of the most useful sites, and one you will want to return to on a regular basis, is the FMLM (www.fmlm.ac.uk). In 2010, The Royal College of Physicians (London) and the Royal College of General Practitioners organised a meeting in collaboration with other bodies, including the AMRC, the NHS Institute for Innovation and Improvement and NHS Employers to consider setting up the FMLM, and it was formally endorsed the following year by the AMRC. Leadership and management support is available for individual and team development as well as for organisations. There is ample information about a range of courses. Some of these are generic in nature whilst others are specialty specific, such as the *Surgical Leader Programme*. There is also a good range of publications as well as the *BMJ Leader*, a quarterly journal and the official journal of the FMLM.

The NHS Leadership Academy is also an extremely useful site (www.leadershipacademy.nhs.uk). This has useful tools and resources, but with regards to training and development, the focus is on developmental programmes. There are also several highly respected programmes for different stages of leadership development. For those new to medical leadership and management, the *Edward Jenner Programme* is a good place to start. For those aiming for a more senior management role, the *Nye Bevan Programme* would be more suitable. As an illustration, the *Nye Bevan Programme* runs over 12 months and involves a combination of online work, self-directed learning, several residential workshops as well as a *viva* assessment. It is an excellent programme, but even with an NHS subsidy, the current cost is £7000! You'll have to use all your management and negotiation skills to get this approved.

Most universities also provide a wide range of leadership courses and qualifications, and many have whole departments devoted to the subject. Not all courses are relevant to those in the health sector, so you'll need to explore these carefully. As an example, the University of Keele (www.keele.ac.uk) provides excellent management and leadership training. There is a good range of courses for those working in the healthcare sector, including courses for one or several days, Certificates, Diplomas and degree-level qualifications. These are now well established at Keele and are organised by the *Keele Clinical Leadership Academy*. The *Postgraduate Certificate in Healthcare Leadership and Management* is particularly popular. Participants will be expected to complete a certain number of specified *modules* and be awarded the requisite number of *credits* in order to receive their qualification. The time taken to achieve these will determine how long the course (for you) will take. The three main qualifications are *Certificates*, *Diplomas* and *Master's* degrees. These are all at the same educational level (Level 7) in the National Qualifications Framework, but each takes a different amount of time to complete. As a very rough rule of thumb, Certificates take 15 weeks full-time equivalent (fte), Diplomas 30 weeks fte and Master's degrees 1 year fte. It is sometimes possible to transfer credits from a Diploma to a Master's, or if your circumstances have changed and you are unable to complete your Master's degree, to be awarded a Diploma or Certificate, depending on the number of credits you have accumulated. This is only a guide and you'll need to check the specific requirements and rules for individual universities and courses. These are all taught postgraduate qualifications. For those of you who really want to push your training (and qualifications) in medical leadership and management, there are also research-based opportunities, including doing a PhD!

The variety and range of courses available emphasise the need to think carefully about your leadership and management training and development, not to rush into training but to undertake a careful TNA.

The emphasis here has been on taught courses but it is also important to gain practical experience in medical leadership and management, and these should be linked together over time and be central to your development as a leader. This experience is likely to come, in the main, from working in your own organisation, but it can also be acquired from contributing to other bodies such as your own Royal College, a local university department and regional offices of Health Education England as well as other national bodies such as the GMC and the CQC. You can contribute and chair meetings (eg Medical Staff Committee, Medical Education Committee, Drug and Therapeutic Committee), contribute to and/or lead on small and specific management projects (eg implementation plans following external reviews, introduction of electronic patient records) and larger projects such as service transformations and estate developments for clinical service. There is usually no shortage of things to contribute to gain experience AND make a genuine and meaningful contribution to your service and organisation. However, it is important not to take on too much, to discharge your commitments and to finish what you have agreed and to try and link what you have agreed with your personal development. You should also discuss your experiences and be open to constructive criticism, collect feedback from colleagues as part of the appraisal process and be prepared to change and develop. You can do this through a variety of means including formal supervision, reflection (personal and group) and learning sets (Chapter 5) as well as coaching and mentoring (Chapter 5).

LEADERSHIP AND DEVELOPMENT OVER TIME

Senior doctors have traditionally been thrown in at the 'deep end' after training when it comes to medical leadership and management, and knowledge and skills have had to be acquired 'on the job'. However, contributing to the leadership agenda in an organisation is one of the most important roles senior doctors will have, and yet they are often poorly prepared for the challenge, potentially putting themselves at risk of making significant mistakes and exposing them to 'exploitation' – don't agree to things in corridors!

There are a range of roles in medical leadership and management and some of these have been discussed in Chapter 1, and the main roles and responsibilities of the Medical Director are summarised in Table 1.2. The terminology can be confusing and although Medical Director and Deputy Medical Director have a consistency of meaning across services, other terms such as Associate Medical Director, Clinical Director, Programme Director, Clinical Lead and Head of Service will vary across organisations and over time. When applying for a leadership role or aiming to develop your knowledge and skills for a particular role, it makes sense to focus on the key aspects of the role, usually outlined in a job description. The authors advocate a developmental approach to acquiring the knowledge and skills required for leadership roles, rather than attending a series of 'random' courses in the hope that this, over time, will equip you with the skills and knowledge you need and as such it's important to plan your training. The approach used for clinical development is a good model. Training and development should to be over time, and although there will be a specific period of training and development, it needs to be 'life long learning'. There should be experience of both practical and academic aspects, with opportunities for contemporaneous feedback, reflection and learning. Your organisation should support your educational and training needs, but you also need to ensure these are aligned with the needs of your organisation so you can both benefit.

You'll need to think about the competences you want to achieve at different stages of your career and have a process in place to access these. The advantage of the various programmes provided by the NHS Leadership Academy is that all this is done for you – you can choose the most appropriate programme for your current level of experience and then progress through the programmes to the level that is most appropriate to your needs. The importance of having well-trained and experienced medical leaders in the NHS and the healthcare sector is now well recognised. However, compared with only a few years ago, it's unlikely that you'll be appointed to a senior leadership and management role without evidence of good quality training in this area and, increasingly, a formal qualification.

CONCLUSIONS

The next few years will be an exciting time for medical leadership in the NHS and healthcare sector. There is now a much greater recognition of the importance and the need for doctors to be properly trained in medical leadership so they can make the best possible contribution to the leadership agenda. There have been a lot of changes in medical education and training in recent years, and it is very gratifying to know that junior trainees are now expected to develop leadership skills. This is now extended throughout the period of training and the OOPE scheme is a wonderful example of this. Senior doctors also need to support trainees and junior colleagues to develop their management and leadership skills and formally evaluate these. For those in substantive posts, there are many obstacles to training and development, and this chapter has outlined how these can be negotiated and overcome. It has also provided a flavour of some of the ways to access training and gain practical experience in medical leadership. The key point is to plan your training needs carefully so you can make best use of your time and other resources. Your training and development should also support your organisation to deliver safe and effective patient care within a well-developed and managed service so that everyone benefits.

REFERENCES

1. General Medical Council (2009) *Tomorrow's Doctors; Outcomes and Standards for Undergraduate Medical Education.* https://www.gmc-uk.org/Tomorrow_s_Doctors_1214.pdf_48905759.pdf (accessed 8 January 2018).
2. Department of Health (2002) *Unfinished Business; Proposals for Reform of the Senior House Officer Grade.* http://webarchive.nation-alarchives.gov.uk/20110929193926/http://www.dh.gov.uk/prod_consum_dh/groups/dh_digitalassets/@dh/@en/documents/digitalasset/dh_4018808.pdf (accessed 8 January 2018).
3. General Medical Council (2012) *Leadership and Management for All Doctors.* https://www.gmc-uk.org/guidance (accessed 8 January 2018).
4. Covey SR (2012) *The 7 Habits of Highly Effective People.* New York: Simon & Schuster.
5. Skillnets (2013) *Training Needs Analysis (TNA) Guide.* https://www.skillnets.ie/sites/skillnets.ie/files/imce/u7/tna_guide_2013.pdf. (accessed 8 January 2018).
6. Academy of Medical Royal Colleges and NHS Institute for Innovation and Improvement (2010) *The Medical Leadership Competency Framework.* https://www.fmlm.ac.uk/resources/medical-leadership-competency-framework (accessed 8 January 2018).
7. Bagnall P (2012) *Facilitators and Barriers to Leadership and Quality Improvement.* London, UK: The King's Fund Junior Doctor Project, The King's Fund.

11

Balance

YOUR MOST IMPORTANT ASSET IS YOURSELF

Some leaders and senior managers succeed in their careers only at the expense of a wrecked personal life. Others wreck their personal lives without being markedly successful at work! Somehow, some succeed at both. Balance is essential if anybody is going to survive and thrive as a medical manager and leader. The practice of medicine is stressful and being a medical manager and leader, often with additional clinical responsibilities, is probably even more stressful. One maladaptive response to stress is excessive alcohol consumption; another is spending too much time at work whilst ignoring efficiency and effectiveness. You can probably think of others.... In this chapter, we are going to use some approaches from coaching to demonstrate more-adaptive responses.

UNDERSTANDING YOUR NEEDS

Sometimes we suffer from 'superhero syndrome'. We think we can neglect our own humanity and health needs and still perform at a high level. We may be able to do this for a while in an emergency but trying to do it habitually is a recipe for disaster. So, what are our needs? The same as any human being, doctors and doctor-managers have

- Physical needs
- Emotional and relationship needs
- Mental and intellectual needs
- Aesthetic, creative and expressive needs
- Spiritual needs

Covey, Merrill and Merrill [1] express these same needs in the memorable phrase that people need 'to Live, to Love, to Learn and to Leave a Legacy'. In coaching practice, when somebody reports they are getting bad-tempered and 'cranky' at work, the coach sees this as a possible signal that important needs are not getting met. There are two polar opposite approaches to needs. At one extreme, people may be obsessed with their needs to the point that they think of little else and may make little contribution to society (characterized as narcissistic in some typologies). At the other, people deny their needs and end up feeling very stressed and perhaps using maladaptive coping strategies. In the experience of the authors, most doctors and doctor-managers tend to deny their needs, often resulting in under-functioning or unhappiness. According to Coppock [2], when we recognise that we are being 'driven' or affected by an unmet need, there are two complementary approaches we can take. We can either change our attitude so that the 'need' is no longer so important or we can do what we can to meet the need. Which approach we take depends, to some extent, on the nature of the need and our circumstances at the time. The need to eat an adequate but not excessive diet can, for example, only be put on one side briefly without serious health consequences! The need for exercise, however, permits a wider range of adaptive behaviours.

Physical needs

How much time do you give to physical renewal or maintenance? Diet, exercise and rest are all important to our physical and psychological well-being. How many doctors skip lunch or nibble unhealthy food at their desks rather than taking a time away from the office, surgery, theatre, ward or consulting room for a nutritious lunch and brief relaxation? Exercise is often hard to find time, for but there are many ways to approach this. For some, cycling to work at least 1 or 2 days per week may be a good option. Even parking the car a good distance from the workplace and walking briskly, using stairs rather than lifts can help. For others being part of a sports or dance team or playing golf or going to the gym may do the trick. The key is finding something that works for you and that you can sustain on a regular basis. What about relaxation and sleep? How many doctor-managers lie awake at night trying to resolve impossible problems? You may need to learn to relax so that you can keep your blood pressure down and get off to sleep.

Emotional and relationship needs

We have already discussed the importance of good-quality relationships and emotional 'intelligence' in the workplace (Chapters 2 and 9). Our needs for companionship, fun, mutual understanding, appreciation and respect and our need to contribute to the well-being of others extend well beyond the workplace, and it is these needs that we want to consider here. By the time they rise to more senior management roles, most doctors will have been in a number of close adult relationships. They may be married; they may have children. These relationships can be a source of great balance and support, but they also need input of time and energy to maintain them. We need to be able to give to others and to receive from them. Covey [3] writes of 'the emotional bank account' – our reciprocal emotional 'credit' line with our partners and others. To give to others, we need to have confidence in our own status. If we feel empty, we find it hard to give more. And here lies one of the dangers of a demanding job. If we leave work feeling 'drained', it may be hard to give our partner and/or our children the love they need. By being ever-giving at work, we run the risk of becoming ever-needy at home. We need to make a conscious effort to keep a balance in our lives between work and home. This means keeping work and personal life within explicit boundaries. We need to be explicit with other people at work and at home about setting up agreed boundaries that work for all parties.

Prolonged stress can lead to underperformance and mental ill health; Chapter 9 offers more support in this area.

Mental and intellectual needs

Intellectual rigour is a value that is important to all the authors. It is based on a need to understand things thoroughly. This can find expression in scientific research, in psychodynamic understanding, in teaching, in writing and, of course, in clinical and managerial work. A number of other needs can be listed in this domain:

- Stimulation from reading and interaction
- Satisfying curiosity in a rigorous way
- Learning new things
- Solving problems
- Planning
- Being in control of one's own life and work
- Having an ordered existence
- The search for meaning (which can also be regarded as a key part of the spiritual domain)

Most doctors will have spent a good part of their lives reading and interacting with others in gaining the competences needed for their work; but what about reading 'outside the box' not only for recreation but also as a way of throwing new light on our professional lives? Good biographies can be inspirational and books on psychology (and, dare we say it, some management books) may help us understand ourselves and our working environment better. Being in control of one's own life and work and having an ordered existence are important needs for many people and lack of control over one's own life at work (or at home) is a frequent source of stress and unhappiness. Many doctors and doctor-managers will find that their intellectual needs can at least be partly satisfied by properly structuring their time at work. Research and audit are examples of parts of the doctor's work life that can be conducted with intellectual rigour and be a source of new learning and problem-solving.

Aesthetic, creative and expressive needs

If you are blessed with creative talent, use it. Some people draw or paint or take wonderful photographs, some sing, dance or play a musical instrument and some write books and develop new ideas. Try not to frustrate such needs through lack of time, but seek to devote proper time and attention to them. For some people, simply seeing a great work of art or being in beautiful mountain scenery may satisfy deep aesthetic needs. Here again, some people would link this with a sense of meaning in a separate 'spiritual' domain.

Spiritual needs

These are not recognised by everybody. For some people, they may be subsumed under mental and intellectual needs. For others, these needs may be satisfied by adherence to a formal religion, way or path. The kind of things that may be included are listed here:

- Inspiration
- Meaning and purpose
- Quiet connecting time
- Time in nature
- Gratitude and celebration
- Kind actions and generosity of spirit

For more on this area, see *Spiritually Competent Practice in Health Care* [4].

EXERCISE 11.1
Needs review

Consider your needs. This needs review (Table 11.1) is modified from *The Self Factor* [2] with permission. It is not a test with psychometric validity. Rather, it is an inventory to facilitate the reader making a judgement about how far they are meeting their own needs in different areas. The instructions with the original review are as follows:

When you have completed the needs review (in Table 11.1), choose two or three (or more) that you would like to meet more fully. For each one, ask yourself the following questions and write down your replies:

- How do I feel when this need is not being met?
- How do I feel when this need *is* being met?
- What difference would it make if I took better care of this need?
- What are the implications if I continue not to take care of it?
- What would be involved in getting this need met more fully?

(Continued)

> **EXERCISE 11.1 (Continued)**
>
> - How would I like things to be in 3 months and what is achievable?
> - What steps can I take this week to start to improve things?
> - What support do I need to make this a sustainable change?
>
> Now start to make changes. Remember that the journey of a thousand miles begins with the first step. So, take the first steps now, whether they are tiny steps or huge strides.

Table 11.1 Needs review

Needs Review **Score *each item on a scale of 1 to 4* according to how you** **feel about it and don't compare yourself to how you think** **it should be.**		**Total**
Physical needs	Rest and relaxation … … … … … ___ Exercise … … … … … … … … … … ___ Touch and sexuality … … … … … ___ Diet … … … … … … … … … … … ___ Healthy Environment ___	TOTAL __/20
Emotional and relatedness needs	Companionship … … … … … … … … ___ Listening and understanding … … … ___ Contributing to others … … … … …. … ___ Fun and recreation … … … … … … … ___ Appreciation and respect … … … … ___	TOTAL __/20
Cognitive and mental needs	Stimulating conversation … … … … … ___ Problem solving … … … … … … … ___ Planning, control and order… … … … ___ Stimulating reading and so on … … … ___ Curiosity/new learning … … … … … ___	TOTAL __/20
Aesthetic, creative and expressive needs	Beauty in environment … … … … … … ___ Creating things or ideas … … … … … ___ Making a difference in the world … ___ Appreciating the arts, music, theatre ___ Self-expression/performance … … ___	TOTAL __/20
Spiritual needs	Gratitude/celebration … … … … … … ___ Time in nature ___ Kind actions and generosity of spirit ___ Prayer/meditation/quiet time … … ___ Inspiration, meaning and purpose … ___ Grand total	TOTAL __/20 __/100

Source: Coppock, D., *The Self Factor*, Findhorn Press, Findhorn, UK, 2005.

Another way to look at the whole question of needs is to imagine yourself as a huge container. Into the container flow all your energy gains: all the things that sustain you physically, mentally and spiritually. Out of the container flow all the things that take energy out of your personal system. Some of these things are legitimate 'output'; things you want to contribute and achieve for yourself, for your friends and family and for your patients and employers. Some of the output goes down the waste pipe! These 'drains' are activities that do not add to your contribution (spending time doing things that really could and *should* be done by others, for example). Making sure all your needs are met is the way to maximise the inflow. Plugging the drains is the way to ensure maximum contribution and achievement. Using this metaphor emphasises that it is a mistake to neglect the 'input' side of the equation. If we do, we soon run out of energy for the outputs!

EXERCISE 11.2
A review of your energy balance

Energy gains, outputs and drains. Make a list in two columns. In one, put the main things that energise you. In the other, put the main things that you use your energy on. Start with the main outputs that you want to maintain, then draw a line and list underneath it all the things that drain energy unprofitably from your personal system. Your list may look something like Table 11.2.

Table 11.2 Energy gains, outputs and drains

Energy gains	Energy output
Personal fitness, diet, exercise and so on	**Useful Outputs**
	Clinical work well done
Family relationships	Management work well done
Walking the dog	Good family relationships
Doing a really good piece of work thoroughly	Keeping fit
	Contribution to running local clubs, church and so on
Some friendships in the local club/pub/ church and so on	Writing a book
Reading a great novel	**Energy Drains**
Writing a book	Using an inefficient computer system at work
	Having to do work that should be done by someone else (especially if that work does not demand your unique skills and competences)
	Reading a badly written report
	Attending useless meetings

One thing is immediately apparent in the container metaphor; it is the drains that create the imbalance. Many positive outputs are energising in themselves. Life is not a 'zero-sum game' [5]. The next thing is how important it becomes to develop plans to deal with the drains and not simply to put up with them. So, if you have completed this exercise for yourself, make a plan to get rid of the energy drains, starting with the easiest and working systematically through the rest!

THE WORK ENVIRONMENT

This is something many doctors tend to neglect. We thought it might be different when new hospitals were built in the UK in the early part of the twenty-first century, but for many senior doctors, getting an office is still an achievement and concerns about adequate support increase. Just as the issues of quality for patients can be divided into clinical effectiveness, safety and patient experience, so the issues of the environment for the health service manager can be divided into

- Effective management systems
- Adequate personal space
- Health and safety
- Quality of the manager's experience of working in the organisation

Effective management systems

This depends on the effectiveness of the organisation, its culture and the technical and administrative support it offers its managers (and clinicians). Enough is now known about appropriate and effective management cultures that no organisation has an excuse for ineffectiveness. See, for example, the Virginia Mason Production System (VMPS) described in Chapter 8. How often in healthcare do we still come across inadequate technical and administrative support systems? Certainly, in the mental health sector of the National Health Service (NHS) there is often insufficiently good management of administration. Clinical letters are still not always standardised (either in headings for content or in timeliness). Electronic record systems are sometimes better at hiding important clinical information than at making it easily accessible. The performance of clerical and administrative support staff is not always properly developed or managed. All these things affect the performance of clinicians and managers.

Adequate personal space

Most people need some place to call their own, even at work. An office that is pleasantly furnished and reasonably quiet is a good starting place. Some people will feel content with a shared office, provided there is easy access to an adequate room for private conversations. Doctors with management roles will often have separate clinical and managerial offices and this helps in separating out management from clinical time by making a physical separation of locations. This cannot be taken for granted. A recent fashion for 'agile working' has seen some doctors relocated away from support services and expected to carry a trolley with their laptop in it from venue to venue ('hot-desking'). One of the authors works at a Trust where 'agile working' was introduced over a year ago, and this has degraded the quality of his workplace experience. Despite holding responsible managerial and clinical posts, he no longer has an office to work from. There is nowhere to store reference books and there is very little personal space, resulting in a noisy and disruptive environment. This makes work more stressful and less efficient than it used to be and also causes problems when confidential conversations are needed as rooms have to be arranged in advance.

People vary in how much they personalise their work-space. What is important is to make sure that the arrangements you have help to sustain you and improve your efficiency and effectiveness.

Health and safety

Issues like comfortable chairs that avoid back strain, appropriate desk space and suitably arranged personal computers that provide a comfortable and safe working area are important. Most organisations offer a workstation assessment for those who spend a lot of their time at a computer or desk. Simple advice on posture, layout of the workstation and suitable chairs can make a positive contribution to well-being and comfort in the workplace. Respect for fire regulations is obviously important. Perhaps less obvious are issues like the risks in home visits, especially 'out of hours', poorly lit car parks and so on.

Quality of experience

This depends on organisational culture and systems efficiency. The NHS has become infamous for a 'bullying culture' in management [6]. This is inimical to effective healthcare. Respect for everyone in the organisation is vital not only for moral reasons but also because it gets the best performance out of people and ensures that good ideas are not wasted [7]. Efficient systems are something the NHS has historically been notoriously bad about in both primary and secondary care. In primary care, a disturbing example was the loss of nearly three quarters of a million items of patient-related correspondence by NHS Shared Business Services (a joint venture between the Department of Health and a private company) which was the subject of a National Audit Office Investigation [8]. In secondary care, as reported in the first edition of this book, there have been reports of a consultant psychiatrist being asked to conduct outpatient consultations in an unconverted bathroom in a 'community outpost'. In the 'agile working' experiment described earlier, issues like the availability of essential office equipment (eg photocopiers) and car parking for those with duties on several sites were not properly considered. Office space for managers has traditionally been of a better quality than that for clinicians. Perhaps this tells a tale of the relative values ascribed to management and clinical work in the 'new managerialism' era of the NHS. The examples of NAViGO and VMPS shared in Chapter 8 show how much better things can be done by committed, innovative organisations.

> **EXERCISE 11.3**
> **Audit of your workplace experience**
>
> Conduct an audit of the quality of your workplace experience. Under the headings of Managerial Effectiveness, Personal Space, Health and Safety and Quality of Experience, list the things that are good about your situation and the things that need changing. Prioritise the things that need changing and make plans to tackle the priority issues with a timescale.
> Get started and review progress regularly.

TAKING THE LONGER VIEW

It is tempting always to be dealing with the urgent stuff. This may be genuine urgency, as in the case of clinical emergencies, or manufactured urgency, as in the case of many government-imposed deadlines for change. If, however, we allow all of our time to be taken up with the urgent, we may not find time for those important things that help us to keep going. This applies as much to our needs for a balanced life as to the organisation's need to take a strategic overview. Only if we maintain our own personal fitness and balance, can we do our best for the organisation we serve.

LESSONS FROM TOYOTA

Until recently, nearly all the management lessons from Toyota have been positive ones. Their concepts of 'just-in-time' supply of parts, a flexible, involved, empowered production staff and total emphasis on quality have been admired often and adapted to health provision in the VMPS (Chapter 8). Now there is a new lesson; even one of the best-managed companies in the world can go wrong if it tries to go too far, too fast.

Let us look first at two of the positive lessons:

- Planning the workflow properly.
- Giving the front-line workforce control of quality and incentives to improve it.

The Toyota manufacturing concept starts with the idea that there should be as few detailed performance targets as possible. The approach is dubbed 'management by means' rather than 'management by results' [9]. Overall targets are set for the company, but these are kept to a minimum. Management emphasis is on designing the means of production in collaboration with the 'front-line' workforce, rather than simply going for 'bottom-line' financial targets. Cars are made to order and as they proceed down the production line, each car, by means of sophisticated information control, effectively 'orders' the parts needed for the next stage of manufacture. Stocks of parts are kept to a minimum.

Production-line processes are designed with input from those who work on the production line, and every member of the production team learns the work of the stages of production immediately upstream and downstream. Anybody who thinks of a better way of performing some operation is encouraged to share it, and all workers are empowered to stop production if they spot a quality issue. The overall flow of production is maintained by having 'buffer zones' between sections of production so that stopping one section does not stop the whole line. For much more sophisticated analyses of the Toyota production model see *Profit Beyond Measure* [9] and *Lean Production Simplified* [10], and for more detail of how it has been translated into healthcare practice, see Chapter 8 and Kenney [7,11]. The Virginia Mason Institute Website (https://www.virginiamasoninstitute.org/?gclid=CKm6-OGp99QCFaoW0wodAV4Hlg) is also useful.

EXERCISE 11.4

Improving the area of work you have responsibility for

How could 'management by means' improve the area of work you carry (some) management responsibility for? What are the simple, obvious things that need putting right? Administrative and clerical support and effective, efficient, well-maintained computer systems come to mind as we write this; but you may have many other suggestions. Choose an area that will make a real difference to performance, and work with key stakeholders to develop a change strategy for it, based on the steps in Chapter 8. Turn this into an action plan (preferably one that is resource neutral) and (with the support of other key players) see it through. Then start on the next priority. Of course, you could go further and persuade your organisation to take on the VMPS.

The more recent lesson from Toyota is that even an almost uniquely well-managed company can go wrong if it tries to do too much, too quickly. Various safety scares in 2010, 2011 and 2016 [12] have damaged the reputation of the company, but it still seems to be maintaining profitability, demonstrating its underlying resilience.

Two examples from Chapter 8, that of NAViGO and VMPS, also emphasise that even successful innovation is not without its challenges. NAViGO, despite building excellent, value-for-money services, found that the Clinical Commissioning Group (effectively the 'customer') was interested in 'average' services and cost-cutting under the pressure of Government austerity policies (see Chapter 8). Virginia Mason [11] found there was a great tendency for agreed innovations to revert to previous practice without constant reinforcement, especially in the early stages of introducing the VMPS.

KEEPING FRESH FOR THE LONG TERM

How do you keep up to date as a manager? We have discussed continuing professional development as a leader and manager in Chapter 10. Here we are more concerned with day-to-day self-maintenance. Having management colleagues one can easily approach to discuss difficult issues is important. Another useful way of keeping fresh is to have a 'peer group' of managers who can act as a forum for regular discussion of issues and sharing of ideas. Medical Directors may have (or be able to form) a local cohort of Medical Directors who can help them. Clinical Directors and those in similar roles may band together to better develop their understanding.

In addition to support in the workplace, reading good management books (especially ones that are based on research, experience and observation) is helpful. Books that have survived into two or more editions are also often particularly worthwhile, though not necessarily 'cutting edge'. Some of the authors' favourites are cited throughout and appear in reference lists at the end of chapters. Active, intelligent discussion with other leaders and managers, medically qualified or not, is useful. Conferences, courses and peer groups can facilitate this kind of discussion and can be arranged as a result of a Training Needs Analysis as part of the Personal Development Plan discussed in Chapter 10.

Reflection, conversation and writing

Some would argue that the capacity for reflection is one of the important defining qualities of humanity. When we reflect, we effectively carry out a conversation in our own heads! We discuss things with ourselves, taking time to assess the situation we are concerned with, to consider other people's views, ponder alternatives and (when appropriate) to form action plans. Coaching is really just having another person to 'hold the space' and perhaps provide some structure for this conversation. In fact, this 'holding space' for reflection is perhaps the most valuable aspect of coaching. In coaching, however, the conversation is not entirely internal. The coach contributes in many ways including by asking questions, keeping the person to their intention and supporting the formation of action plans. It is amazing how having another person listening, but not telling us what they think we should do, can help the process.

Another way of helping reflection is to write down our thoughts in a structured way. This includes things like the balance wheel in Chapter 1; the time-management grid in Chapter 5; the use of a structure such as Whitmore's 'GROW' (Goal, Reality, Options and Will) acronym, mentioned in Chapter 4; the personal needs inventory discussed in this chapter; keeping a reflective diary (and even writing books!). You may have great skill in reflecting on your experience, but if you have not tried working with a coach or writing things down in some structured way, you should think about it and try it.

WISDOM

Wisdom involves the ability to make decisions, based on knowledge, experience, reflection, sound values and good judgement. It has been prized since ancient times and the Old Testament King Solomon was famous for it. In the setting of health service management, wisdom often consists in finding a way through the tangle of political initiatives, bureaucracy, regulation and targets to deliver first, what is good for the patient; second, what is good for the organisation; and third, what is good for the people who work in it. In an ideal world, of course, the way to these three goods and the good of wider society would be identical. In our less-than-ideal world, the patient should come first! Wisdom is seen in many behaviours, for example in responding to situations after reflection, not reacting immediately (unless, of course, an immediate reaction is imperative or life-saving). Wisdom tends to take account of other people's views and tries to reflect on how things really are rather than accepting a distorted view fed to it by one party or another.

Knowing when to stop, change or say 'no'

One aspect of wisdom is knowing when to stop. We are coming to the end of this book. Careers in medical management also come to an end. One of the authors retired from a Medical Director post in a large community and mental health trust partly because he thought the Chief Executive of the Trust had been badly treated and partly because he couldn't put up any longer with the continual political meddling in the NHS. After 5 years pursuing his career as a clinical academic, he 'retired' from clinical work but soon found himself invited to help with medical management in several NHS Trusts with medical management issues. He also trained and worked as a coach, mainly working with doctors in management and trained doctors in coaching and appraisal skills. Now he is largely bowing out of management practice and coaching to focus on his academic interest in old-age psychiatry, medical management and spirituality in healthcare. Knowing when to stop is not easy. One vital aspect for younger medical managers is to make sure that they remain competent clinicians with a guaranteed route back into full-time clinical practice.

Hopefully, some of you reading this are just making a start in medical management and have many years of management development, enjoyment, success and, perhaps, a little failure to learn from ahead. We trust you will give yourself to the task in a balanced way that will preserve your sanity, your family relationships and friendships and that you will know when to step off the management 'ride' even if it is not until you retire or later.

REFERENCES

1. Covey S, Merrill A and Merrill R (1994) *First Things First*. London, UK: Simon & Schuster.
2. Coppock D (2005) *The Self Factor*. Findhorn, UK: Findhorn Press.
3. Covey S (2004) *7 Habits of Highly Effective People*. London, UK: Simon & Schuster.
4. Wattis J, Curran S and Rogers M (Eds) (2017) *Spiritually Competent Practice in Health Care*. Boca Raton, FL: CRC Press.
5. Wright R (2001) *Nonzero*. London, UK: Abacus.
6. Johnson S (2016) NHS staff lay bare a bullying culture. *The Guardian*. https://www.theguardian.com/society/2016/oct/26/nhs-staff-bullying -culture-guardiansurvey (accessed 2 May 2018).

7. Kenney C (2015) *Virginia Mason's Story: A Leadership Journey in Healthcare*. Boca Raton, FL: CRC Press.
8. National Audit Office (2017) *Investigation: Clinical Correspondence Handling at NHS Shared Business Services*. London, UK: NAO.
9. Johnson HT and Broms A (2000) *Profit Beyond Measure*. New York: Simon & Schuster.
10. Dennis P (2015) *Lean Production Simplified*. Boca Raton, FL: CRC Press.
11. Kenney C (2011) *Transforming Health Care: Virginia Mason Medical Center's Pursuit of the Perfect Patient Experience*. Boca Raton, FL: CRC Press.
12. Davies R (2016) Toyota recalls nearly 73,000 UK vehicles over safety fears. *The Guardian*. https://www.theguardian.com/business/2016/jun/29/toyota -recalls-34000-ukvehicles-defective-airbag-concerns (accessed 2 May 2018).

FURTHER READING

West MA (2012) *Effective Teamwork: Practical Lessons from Organizational Research*. Oxford, UK: Blackwell Publishing.

Index